Kbor Klib
and the Battle of Zama

Duncan Ross

BAR International Series 1399
2005

Published in 2016 by
BAR Publishing, Oxford

BAR International Series 1399

Kbor Klib and the Battle of Zama

ISBN 978 1 84171 838 5

BAR Publishing is the trading name of British Archaeological Reports (Oxford) Ltd.
British Archaeological Reports was first incorporated in 1974 to publish the BAR
Series, International and British. In 1992 Hadrian Books Ltd became part of the BAR
group. This volume was originally published by Archaeopress in conjunction with
British Archaeological Reports (Oxford) Ltd / Hadrian Books Ltd, the Series principal
publisher, in 2005. This present volume is published by BAR Publishing, 2016.

Printed in England

BAR
PUBLISHING

BAR titles are available from:

       BAR Publishing
       122 Banbury Rd, Oxford, OX2 7BP, UK
EMAIL   info@barpublishing.com
PHONE +44 (0)1865 310431
  FAX   +44 (0)1865 316916
       www.barpublishing.com

Kbor Klib, taken from what is proposed to be the battlefield of Zama, approximately three kilometers due west, in the direction of Seba Biar.

Contents

List of Figures

Acknowledgements

The author conceived the idea of a connection between Kbor Klib and the battle of Zama during a visit to the monument in autumn 2001. Traveling companions Ken and Jane Cundiff indulged the author's enthusiasm. University of Munich Professors Dr. Michael Mackensen, Dr. phil. Hans Baldus and Dr. phil. Jakob Seibert generously offered advice. Former UM Professor Dr. Franz Tinnifeld provided a preliminary introduction to these scholars, and, especially, to the Bavarian State Library. Professor David Mattingly afforded guidance and support during the initial preparation of the paper. Dr. phil. Siegmar von Schnurbein facilitated access to the excellent Römisch-Germanische Kommission facilities in Frankfurt, as well as the opportunity to lecture at Goethe University. Dr. Taher Ghalia kindly provided access to the Artemis shield in the Bardo museum. Dr. Friedrich Rakob tolerantly entertained the author's theories. The Principal Consular Officer at the US Embassy to Tunisia, Nora Dempsey, afforded immeasurable support during the entire process.

Chapter 1
Kbor Klib; its Location and a brief Description;
Previous Investigations

The Monument

In the remote countryside of north-central Tunisia, between the cities of Siliana and Le Kef, stands a ruined stone structure known as Kbor Klib (*Figs. 1 & 2*).

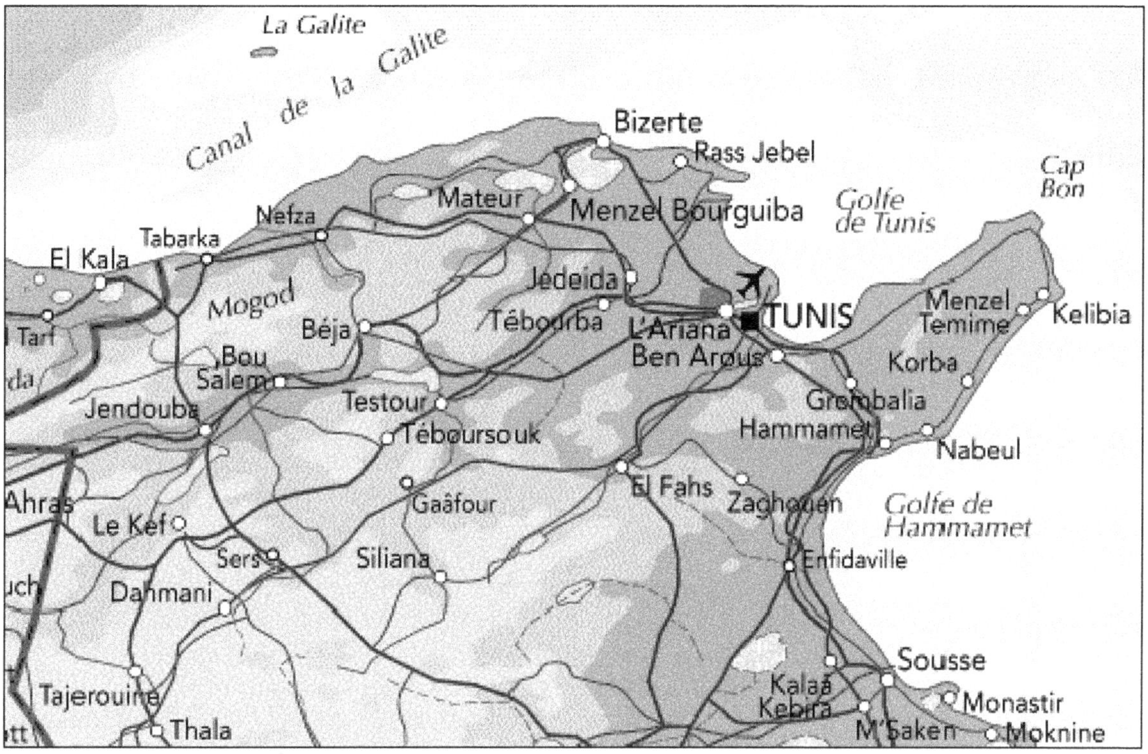

Fig. 1. Northern Tunisia; Kbor Klib is located west of Siliana.

The monument is shown on the more detailed maps of the country and mentioned in the more thorough guidebooks, so the interested visitor knows roughly where and what to expect while traveling the lonely stretch of road near which it lies. Nonetheless, Kbor Klib comes as something of a revelation, isolated on and dominating the ridgeline where it stands. This sense of isolation, of solitary grandeur, is not diminished by closer approach.

The extant structure is oriented lengthwise almost due north-south and measures roughly 45 meters long by ten meters wide, with the highest remaining block some six meters above the base. The stones that compose the exterior of the monument are much degraded, shifted out of position, fallen, or missing altogether. The interior mass of the structure is consequently visible, composed of large, roughly worked stone blocks, with the interstitial spaces filled with broken stones and a distinctive yellow clay (*Fig. 5*).

Excellently finished, tightly jointed facing stones are, however, still in evidence, mainly in the northerly of the two passages that penetrate the monument. These corridors are a principal feature of Kbor Klib, open to the west but blocked on the eastern side (*Fig. 6*). A few scattered, sculpted fragments confirm that some degree of architectural decoration once adorned the structure (*Fig. 7*).

1

To the west are the ruins of another, much smaller construction (*Fig. 3, & Fig. 8*). The size and the weathering of the stones composing this smaller remnant give the immediate impression of an affinity between the two structures. Indeed, the two have the unmistakable feel of a composition, and what is more, a composition focused on the west, on the overlooked countryside. Whatever this composition was, the visitor immediately feels it was intimately connected to the landscape, from which it derived significance, and to which it brought meaning.

These are first impressions, and in this thinly populated terrain, on a windy, cloud-tossed day, it is difficult not to be impressed. Others must surely have contemplated these ruined structures, and this view, and some of them must surely have been moved to more than mere contemplation, must have been moved to investigate. A thorough examination of North African archaeological documentation reveals that, indeed, Kbor Klib has over the years been the subject of a variety of descriptions, discussions and investigations.

Previous Research on Kbor Klib; a Recapitulation

Kbor Klib entered the European written record with a short description by Julien Poinsott in the *Bulletin des Antiquités Africaines* of 1884 (Picard 1957: 208). Cagnat and Saladin, writing in 1887 of their journey through Tunisia, were apparently the next to mention Kobeur-el-Koulib. They described its construction as consisting of "trois pyramides tronquées", and noted that the Tomb of the Christian Woman, located in Algeria and known to the be the sepulcher of the Numidian kings, was also pyramidal in form. They therefore supposed that Kbor Klib must be a mausoleum, most likely for local nobility (Cagnat & Saladin 1887: 260).

Kbor Klib then appeared in 1920 in a one-line description accompanying a map of the area included in the *Atlas Archeologique de la Tunisie*, an exhaustive survey of Tunisian archaeological sites prepared under the aegis of the French colonial administration. Kebour Klib was here described as a "Grand mausolee: fort byzantin", referencing Poinsott. The same atlas page mentioned the site of Ksar Toual Zouameul, located approximately one kilometer to the east of Kbor Klib (*Fig. 2*), and containing a "Beau mausolée bien conservé (*Fig. 9*); inscriptions" (Cagnat). Thus Ksar Toual and Kbor Klib were early on connected in the research, as well as through physical proximity.

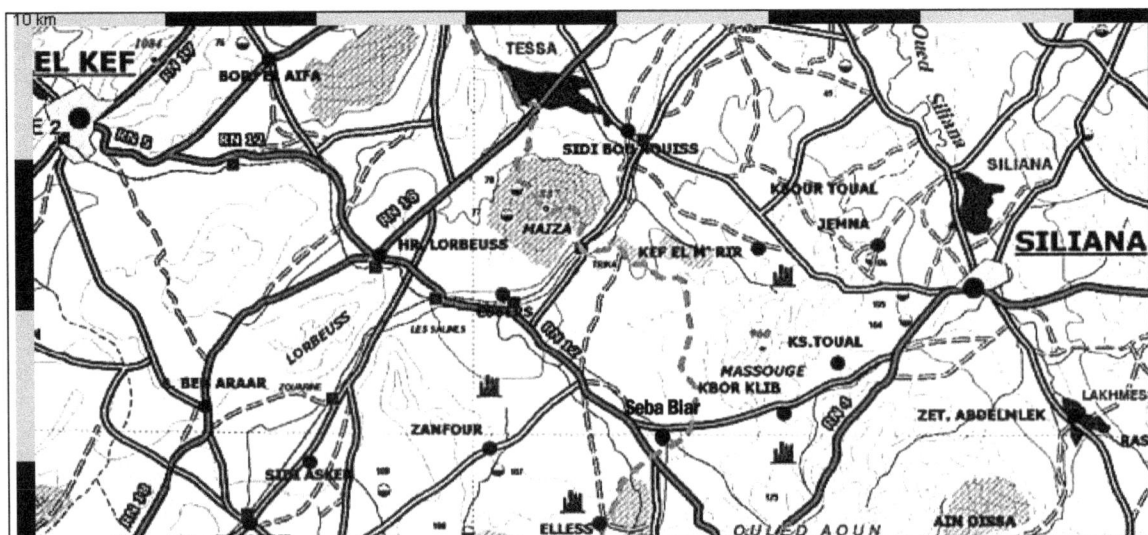

Fig. 2. North Central Tunisia; Kbor Klib SW of Siliana.

Fig. 3. Kbor Klib, looking NE from the SW. Note separate structure to the west.

Fig. 4. View looking SE from the NW, again with separate structure to the west.

Fig. 5. Kbor Klib east side, interior construction.

*Fig. 6. Kbor Klib, west face, center section, showing the two corridors,
with smaller structure in front.*

Fig. 7. Remains of fallen, sculpted cornice block

Fig. 8. Looking down from the top of Kbor Klib on the smaller structure to the west.

Serious speculation regarding Kbor Klib began with an article by Charles Saumagne in the *Revue Tunisienne* of 1941. Some time previous to his article two inscriptions had been discovered at Ksar Toual Zouameul that contained fragments of the name, Zama Regia. Using this epigraphic evidence, combined with documentary information, Saumagne argued that the ruins at Ksar Toual must be the former Numidian royal city of Zama, famous for its connection to the ancient battle of that name. In this article, Saumagne discussed Kbour-bou-Klib, quoting Poinsott's description of the monument as an enormous mausoleum. Also quoting Poinsott, Saumagne noted that the form of Kbor Klib constituted three separate bases, divided by the corridors, these bases surmounted by "trois pyramides". Saumagne proposed that the vast edifice of Kbor Klib must be a "monumentum regium", and therefore somehow connected to royalty.

Saumagne repeated the account, given by Julius Caesar in *The African War*, that Zama Regia had been the capital of the Numidian king Juba 1, who had sided with the Pompeian forces against Caesar during the Roman civil war. When departing for the conflict, Juba had left his wives, children and treasure at Zama. He had also advised the residents that, should the war go against him, he would return, kill the inhabitants, and destroy the city. Naturally enough, when the Pompeian forces were defeated at the battle of Thapsus, on the coast of Tunisia, and Juba fled the field to return to Zama, the citizens refused him entrance. Juba thereupon retired to one of his estates and committed suicide. Caesar, reaching Zama sometime after the battle, rewarded the city by making it the capital of a new Roman province. According to Saumagne, Caesar, upon his arrival, would have authorized the burial of Juba in Kbor Klib, which Saumagne believed to be the Numidian "tombeau dynastique" (1941: 250-251). Thus was born the connection, logically rather tenuous, of Kbor Klib and Julius Caesar. This conjectural connection is still being published (Jacob & Morris 2001: 267).

Saumagne also observed that Ksar Toual (and therefore Kbor Klib) "commande le couloir entre la vallée de la Siliana et la plaine du Sers". He further remarked that from Kbor Klib the vista embraces the Plain of Sers to the west (1941: 242, 250).

At the time of the Saumagne article Ksar Toual, Kbor Klib and the surrounding terrain were the property of August Prenat, who had purchased the land from the French colonial authority. Saumagne noted that the Ksar Toual inscriptions he studied were recovered by Prenat, who was apparently an amateur archaeologist (Saumagne 1941: 241). In February 1947, the *Bulletin Archéologique du Comité des Travaux Historiques et Scientifiques* (*BAC*) reported that Prenat was now excavating Ksar Toual Zouameul, under the auspices of the French "Service des Antiquités", and that he was also carrying out clearances on the superstructure of Kbor Klib. This report noted the Zama Regia inscriptions from Ksar Toual, and mentioned Kbor Klib, repeating the attribution of the structure as a monumental mausoleum (Picard 1947: 229).

The *BAC* for December of 1947 reported that the excavations at both Ksar Toual Zouameul and Kbor Klib had been taken over by a member of l'École française de Rome, Louis Déroche, under the auspices of that organization. This un-illustrated article announced that a number of bas-relief architectural fragments had been recovered at Kbor Klib, "tant dans la fouille de M. Prenat que dans celle de M. Déroche". These fragments included the carven-stone forms of a shield, a sword and a cuirass. The report consequently questioned the identification of Kbor Klib of a mausoleum, and speculated that it might instead have been an "édifice triomphal". The article observed that the Saumagne identification of three pyramids was incorrect, and reported instead that Kbor Klib was formed of three stone cubes rising from a single base. The 1947 article also noted that there were at one time stairs in the passages dividing the monument, which would have permitted access to the top of the monument (Picard 1947: 376-377). The existence of these stairs was confirmed by layout markings scribed on the stones on the insides of both passageways, these markings still evident today (*Fig. 10*).

In 1948, the *Comptes Rendus des Séances de L'Académie des Inscriptions & Belles-Lettres* (*CRAI*) reported "trois campagnes" of excavation by Déroche at Kbor Klib. This un-illustrated article again observed, "Kbor Klib...marque le passage d'un col, entre les bassins de la Siliana et du Sers, dans la région où se dressait certainement...Zama Regia". The report noted that the construction technique used on the monument, of large stones bound by an earthen mortar, was pre-Roman. It noted that the style of fragments of column capitals recovered from Kbor Klib also predated the Roman presence in Africa, and chronologically could be placed at the end of the Punic period, meaning in the period of the destruction of Carthage. The report therefore asserted that Kbor Klib must date between the end of the Punic and the beginning of the Imperial Roman eras (146 B.C. - 46 B.C.) The report referred to the smaller structure in front of Kbor Klib as an altar, "entouré d'une colonnade ionique" (Picard 1948: 421-422).

Fig. 9. Mausoleum at Ksar Toual, one kilometer east of Kbor Klib, looking east.

7

The 1948 *CRAI* report agreed with the 1947 *BAC* observation that Kbor Klib did not appear to have been funerary in nature. However, the connection with Caesar, proposed when the monument was believed to be a mausoleum, was not abandoned. Instead, the cuirass and shield recovered from the excavations were suggested to have been elements of a frieze of arms decorating the three rectangular bases. These three bases were argued to have been constructed at the order of Caesar to bear three colossal statuary groups celebrating his victories in Gaul, Egypt and Africa. Tradition would have denied Caesar the ability to construct a memorial near the location of his victory at Thapsus, as one did not construct on Roman territory monuments celebrating a civil war, and after the civil war Thapsus would have been on Roman territory. However, Zama would have been a suitable location for such a monument, as this was the city which had shut its gates to Juba. Continuing this rather convoluted logic, the report argued that Caesar had taken the idea of a triple trophy from Pompey, who had used the triple trophy theme to commemorate his own three imperial triumphs. Caesar was thus using the symbolism of his former rival for his own aggrandizement. As further support for this argument, the report observed that one of the carven stone shields excavated at Kbor Klib was decorated with the bust of Artemis, and noted that this symbol would have been used on Macedonian shields. Macedonians soldiers had formed the elite of the Egyptian army, and Caesar had recently destroyed that army at Alexandria. Thus, the presence of this eastern Mediterranean motif in the middle of the North African countryside would be explained (Picard 1948: 422-427).

This 1948 *CRAI* report remarked that Kbor Klib was not stylistically unique in North Africa. It observed that the decorations discovered at Kbor Klib closely resembled decorations discovered earlier at the site of a ruined structure near the marble quarries at Chemtou, Tunisia, some 80 kilometers NW of Kbor Klib (*Fig 11*), which also included sculpted stone cuirasses, shields of

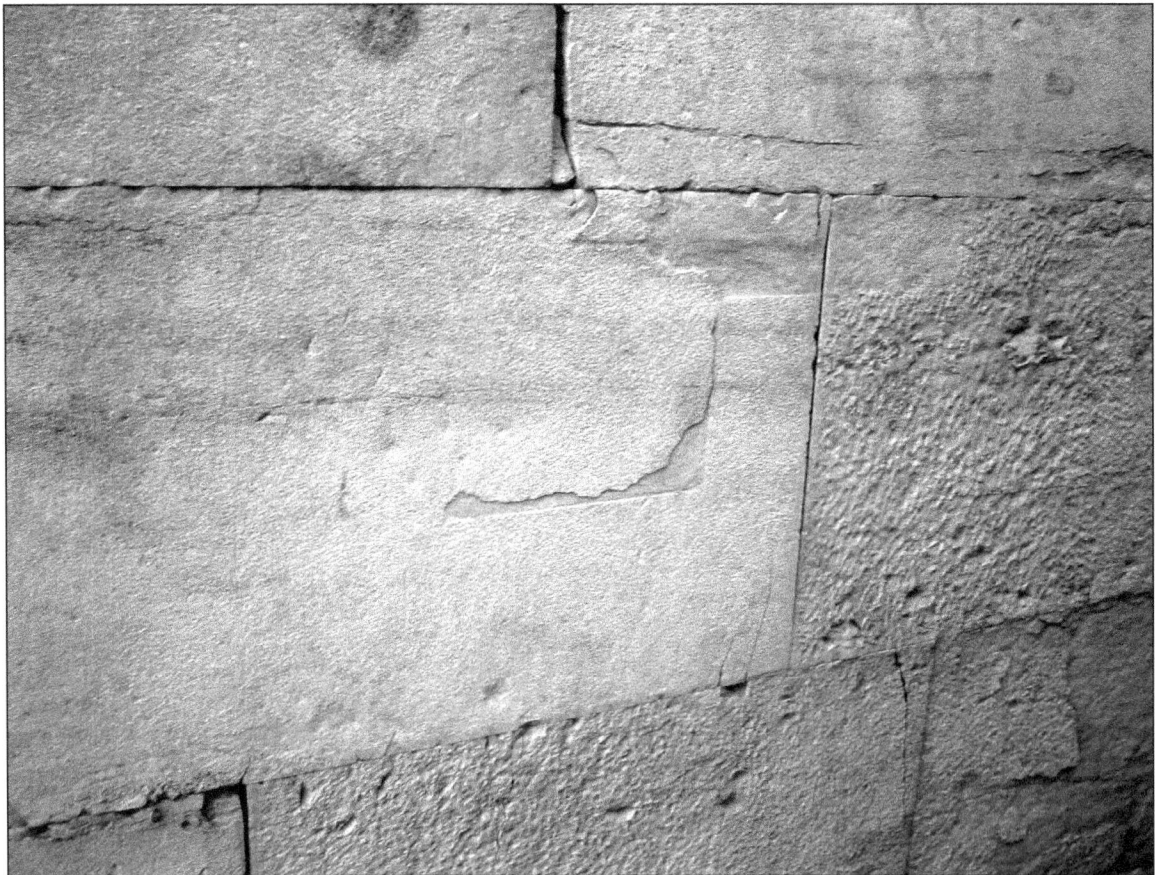

Fig. 10. Stairway layout markings still visible on north wall of north passageway.

the Macedonian type, and weapons (Picard 1948: 423). The structure at Chemtou was, however, significantly smaller than Kbor Klib, measuring 12 meters by 5.5 meters versus the 45 meters by ten meters of Kbor Klib (Picard 1980: 16). Basing the chronology on the style of a recovered column capital, as well as on the use of the Numidian marble taken from the quarries, the report suggested that the monument at Chemtou dated to the first or second centuries B.C. (Picard 1948: 423).

Also in 1948, in the *Mélanges d'Archéologie et d'Histoire de l'École Française de Rome* (*MEFR*), Déroche reported at length on the results of his excavations at Ksar Toual Zammel. He determined that, contrary to Saumagne, Ksar Toual was not Zama Regia, but was instead a relatively insignificant town, the *Vicus Maracitanus*, in the region under the control of Zama Regia (Déroche 1948: 55-85). Déroche noted the proximity of Kbor Klib to Ksar Toual, reporting that the locals considered the monument to be the tomb of a giant, and repeating Saumagne's speculation that perhaps it was the mausoleum of Juba 1 (Déroche 1948: 56).

In 1949 another report on Kbor Klib appeared in the *CRAI*, repeating the identification of the structure as a "trophée monumental". This publication noted that the two passages indenting the structure were open to the west, the side on which "apparement se développait la façade". It again referred to the smaller structure to the west as a large rectangular altar, and again noted that a colonnade would have surrounded this structure, the capitals therefrom recalling Greek models similar to those of Pergamon. Based on this evidence, as well as the stylistic evaluation of the elements from the supposed frieze of arms, this report also concluded that Kbor Klib dated "entre la chute de Carthage et la conquête romaine". The article repeated the identification of Ksar Toual Zammel as the *Vicus Maracitanus*, and not Zama Regia. The report referred to "un fort mémoire de 112 pages, intitulé *Les fouilles du Gbar Klib*" by Déroche (Déroche 1949: 231-232). Unfortunately, it appears that the Déroche report was never published (Picard 1957: 209; Ferchiou 1991: 49).

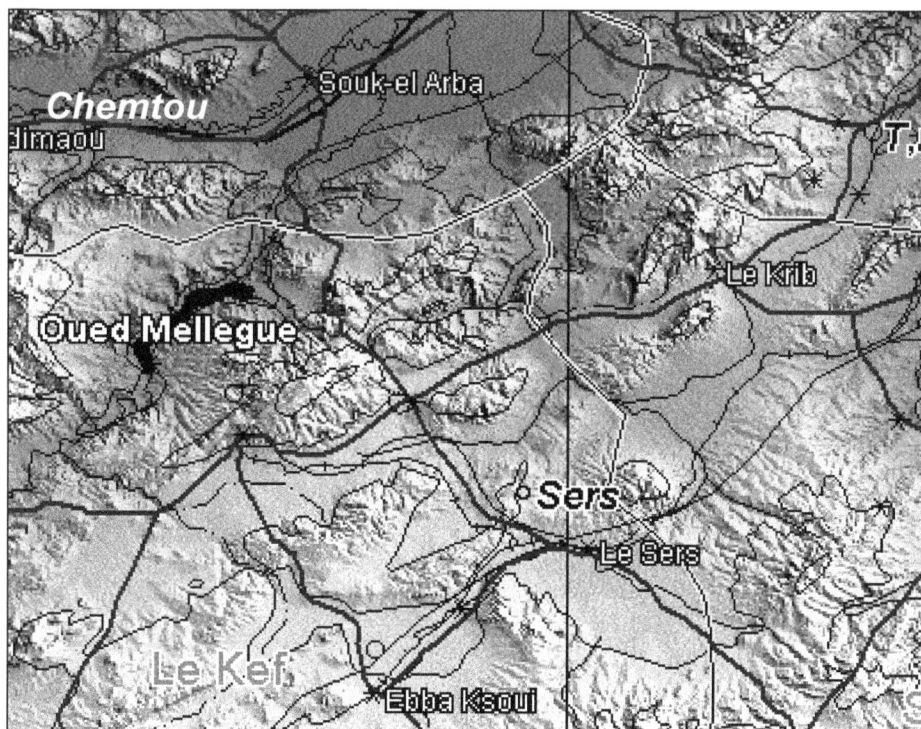

Fig. 11. Chemtou, approx. 80 km NW of Kbor Klib (lower left).

In April 1951 the *American Journal of Archaeology* published one of the few English language descriptions of Kbor Klib. This description consisted of a one-paragraph summary of the Déroche excavations at Kbor Klib, and noted features of the monument including the stairs, the frieze of arms (including the shield with the Artemis head), and the altar. The article observed that the structure was apparently not a tomb, that it predated the imperial period, and that it was likely a monumental trophy (Picard 1951: 192-193).

With this, Déroche disappeared from the scene, and Kbor Klib remained unexcavated for the next 40 years. However, the work of Déroche had been overseen by the archaeologist Gilbert Charles-Picard, at that time Director of Antiquities for Tunisia (Déroche 1949: 231). Picard continued the investigation, and mentioned Kbor Klib a number of times in different contexts and publications over the years following the Déroche excavations. His observations were derived from study of the architectural components recovered by Déroche and Prenat, which had been consigned to the Bardo museum in Tunis, or from examination of the monument itself.

In a 1957 book on Roman battle trophies Picard reiterated the theory that Kbor Klib had been constructed as a triumphal monument during the first century B.C. Picard recognized that the architectural influences for the decoration of Kbor Klib dated from much earlier periods, noting in particular that the shield with the Artemis head was the traditional armor of the hoplite, and that the recovered cuirass was of the Hellenistic type. Indeed, he considered the frieze to have used as its model the reliefs of Pergamon, sculpted at the end of the third or beginning of the second century B.C. The column capitals were similar to ones which had been recently discovered in Carthage, and which appeared stylistically to belong to the last days of that city. A cornice fragment recovered from Kbor Klib also could be stylistically placed in the second century B.C. However, Picard believed that it would have taken time for these architectural styles to infiltrate the interior of North Africa, and that the monument was therefore more recent than these details would indicate. In any case, he asserted that while the pre-Roman Numidian kingdoms may have known of these types of Hellenistic decorations, they were not capable of assembling a monument of the complexity of Kbor Klib. They were, instead, held "a des schémas d'une extrême simplicité" (Picard 1957: 214-216).

While not absolutely denying the possibility of a funerary connection for Kbor Klib, Picard noted the differences of the structure from known North African mortuary monuments in arguing against its attribution as a mausoleum. He reported the marking on the passages which confirmed the former existence of stairs, presumably reaching the top of the structure. He assumed that these stairs indicated that sacrifices must have taken place on the top of Kbor Klib, and remarked "on n'a jamais sacrifié sur un tombeau" (1957: 211). Picard also reported, for the first time, the former presence of doors controlling the passages, the jambs still remaining (Picard 1957: 209).

Picard observed that there was no trace of walls or any other architectural element from the top of the monument. This arrangement, in his opinion, would have only been appropriate for a monumental altar. In further support of this identification Picard noted that Kbor Klib was similar to known monumental altars in other Mediterranean locations, particularly that of a structure built in Syracuse by Hieron II (Picard 1957: 211).

Picard's arguments concerning the reason for the construction of a monumental altar in the middle of the Tunisian countryside are not clearly elucidated. He first observed that the plain of Zama, which he believed to be in the neighborhood of Kbor Klib, was the site of numerous battles, so that construction of a memorial here would not be surprising. However, he then went on to assert that that there had been no event in the history of the pre-Roman Numidian kingdoms which would have warranted a structure as grandiose as Kbor Klib. In his opinion only the Caesarian civil war victory in 46 B.C., on the Tunisian coast, could have justified such a construction. The residents of Zama, having chosen the cause of Caesar over that of their defeated king, would have built Kbor Klib to honor the Roman. Further, although it might have been built by the residents of Zama, thus explaining the indigenous construction technique of rubble and earth fill used for the interior, it must have been Caesar who provided the design, thus explaining the sophistication of the decoration (1957: 214-216). Why Caesar would have directed the use of anachronistic stylistic elements is not explained.

During the course of his discussions Picard argued that Kbor Klib must have been on the territory of the city of Zama Regia, and thus "non loin du célèbre champ de bataille de 202" (Picard 1957: 210). However, his conclusions concerning dating led him to propose that "La chronologie s'oppose donc absolument à ce que nous metions en rapport notre autel avec la bataille de Zama" (Picard 1957: 215). This was the first mention of Kbor Klib in connection with the battle of Zama, as opposed to the town of Zama. With Picard's book, we finally see a plan drawing of the existing condition of Kbor Klib (*Fig. 12*), as well as pictures of some of the recovered elements, including the shield with the Artemis bust (*Fig. 13*), and a cuirass (*Fig. 14*).

The plan view had been produced by Alexandre Lézine, a contemporary of and sometime collaborator with Picard, who independently published on Kbor Klib. Like Picard, Lézine carried out no excavations at Kbor Klib. His research involved examination of the remnants recovered by Déroche and Prenat, or of the monument itself, and the results consisted of short discussions offered while evaluating larger issues, particularly the stylistic development of North African architecture during the classical period. In a 1956 article, entitled "La Maison des Chapiteaux - Histories a Utique", Lézine compared column capital fragments discovered at Kbor Klib with ones from Carthage and from Utica, Tunisia. As had Picard, Lézine reported

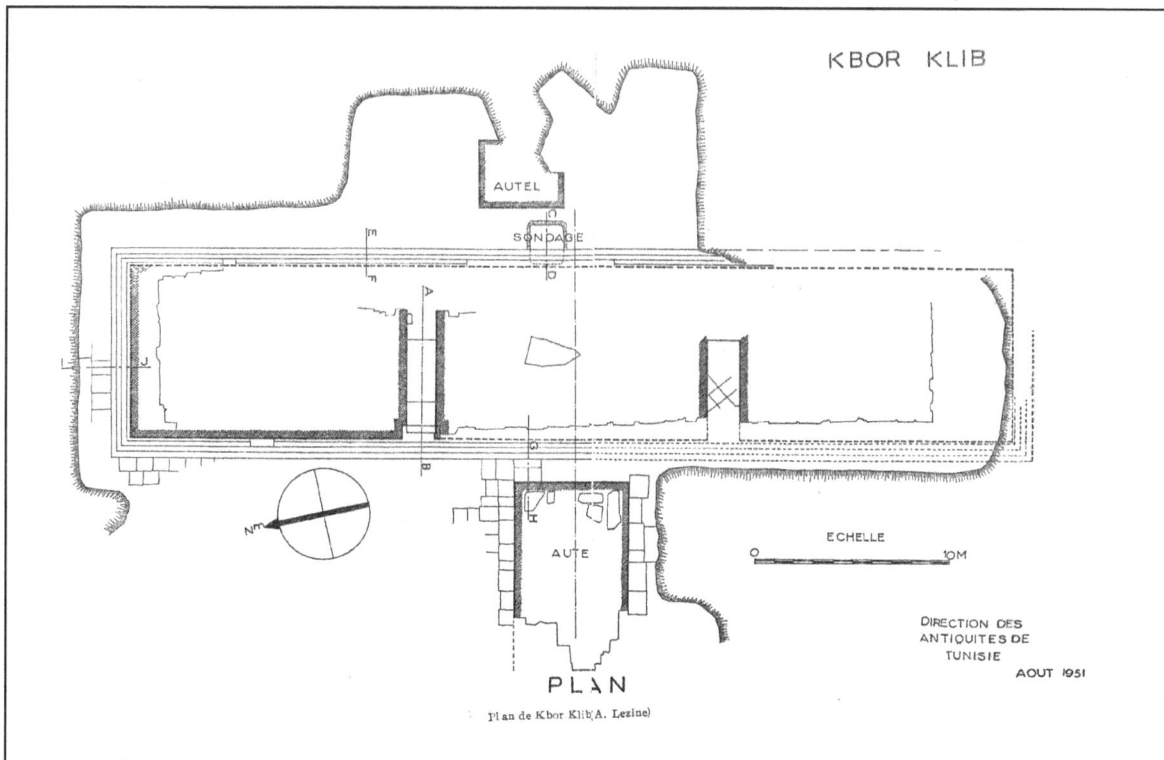

Fig. 12. Plan view drawing of Kbor Klib existing condition.
(Picard 1957: un-numbered figure)

11

similarities between the Kbor Klib and the Carthage examples, and noted that the Carthage capital predated the destruction of that city in 146 B.C. He also noted that the Kbor Klib capital seemed to belong to the same series as the one from Utica, being a possibly more archaic step than the Utica piece in the stylistic development of North African column capitals. The Utica capital he dated to the last quarter of the second century B.C, or the first quarter of the first. However, in a footnote to this report Lézine accepted Picard's dating of 46 B.C., as well as his attribution as a Caesarian monument, for Kbor Klib, (Lézine 1956: 15).

In a 1959 article on triumphal Roman art in the *MEFR* Picard once more referred to Kbor Klib as a triumphal altar, commemorating Caesar's African campaign. He observed that the earlier interpretation of the structure as a series of bases for monumental trophies "doit être abandonée" (Picard 1959: 264)

In a 1962 publication on Punic architecture Lézine again discussed architectural elements recovered at Kbor Klib. In this article, he noted that the capitals from the monument were fundamentally different from those of Utica, implying that they were much older. He went on to evaluate the cornice fragments recovered from Kbor Klib, and after a thorough assessment of the sizes and forms of the pieces he concluded they must date to the second century B.C., and must have been the work of Greek craftsmen. Thus the possibility arose that Kbor Klib might be some 100 years older than the date proposed by Picard and Déroche. In a statement that confirmed his disagreement with Picard, Lézine argued that the archaic form of the cornices could not be explained by cultural retardation, by the backwardness of the Numidian culture responsible for the construction of Kbor Klib. Indeed, regarding the chronology and attribution of Kbor Klib, he noted that "la date de construction est controversée et l'identification encore hypothétique" (Lézine 1962: 113-114).

In a 1967 book on Hannibal, Picard mentioned Kbor Klib as being on the important ancient road from the ancient coastal city of Hadrumetum (present-day Sousse) to the ancient interior city of Sicca (present-day Le Kef). Picard continued to date Kbor Klib to the first century B.C., and again identified it as a monument to the capture of the town of Zama by Caesar. He again dismissed for chronological reasons any connection between Kbor Klib and the battle of Zama (1967: 205-206 & 267).

In a 1968 publication on architecture and urbanism in Carthage and Utica, Lézine included a short article discussing Kbor Klib. He repeated his supposition that, for stylistic reasons, Kbor Klib must date from "bien antérieure à l'époque de César". He took specific exception to Picard's theories regarding the monument, noting that Picard had first identified it as a mausoleum, then as a trophy, then as a monumental altar comparable to those of Pergamon or of Hieron II at Syracuse. Lézine disputed any stylistic resemblance between Kbor Klib and the Pergamon structure, and observed that the only similarity between Kbor Klib and the Hieron II altar was that both structures were lengthened rectangles. He noted that the dual passages divided Kbor Klib into three separate structures, and argued that if one must suppose that sacrifices were carried out on the summit, it would be necessary to see three separate altars, a configuration he considered unlikely. Based on these observations Lézine concluded that "le Kbour Klib ne peut donc pas être un autel". Lézine did introduce a new element into the discourse, observing that a coin of Juba 1 contained the image of a structure divided into three parts, as was Kbor Klib, although he also noted that there was disagreement as to what structure the coin represented (Lézine 1968: 183-185).

Based on evaluation of the layout marking inside the passages, Lézine observed that the stairs could not have continued straight through the passages and reached the summit. They rose at too shallow a pitch, and would have penetrated the eastern side of the monument before reaching the top. Lézine therefore proposed a second flight of stairs, turning at right angles to the first, to allow access to the top of the monument (*Fig. 15*). One of these staircases would have been used to ascend the monument, in Lézine's opinion, while the other would have been used to descend (Lézine 1968: 184).

Lézine offered no opinion regarding the original function of the monument, nor speculated regarding the purpose of the stairs, nor did he propose a reason for the location. He did provide a proposed reconstruction of a section of the west façade of Kbor Klib, which included a second story (*Fig. 16*). In this he also disagreed with Picard, who believed that there were no architectural elements surmounting the structure. With this article Lézine fades from the investigation of Kbor Klib.

In a 1970 article on the battle of Zama, Francis Russell located the town of Zama Regia at Ksar Toual Zouameul, as had Saumagne some 30 year earlier, although he did acknowledge that Déroche disputed Saumagne's conclusions. In his article Russell repeated the story of the suicide of Juba outside the walls of his capital city, following his defeat in the Roman civil war, and noted that Caesar had visited Zama immediately afterwards. Russell remarked the proximity of Kbor Klib to Ksar Toual, agreed with Picard that Caesar had built a "a great monument with statues surrounding it" to commemorate his victory over Juba, and, like Picard, saw Kbor Klib as the remains of that monument (Russell 1970: 128-129).

Fig. 13. Artemis bust on shield. (Picard 1957: Pl. VI)

Fig. 14. Cuirass. (Picard 1957: Pl. VII)

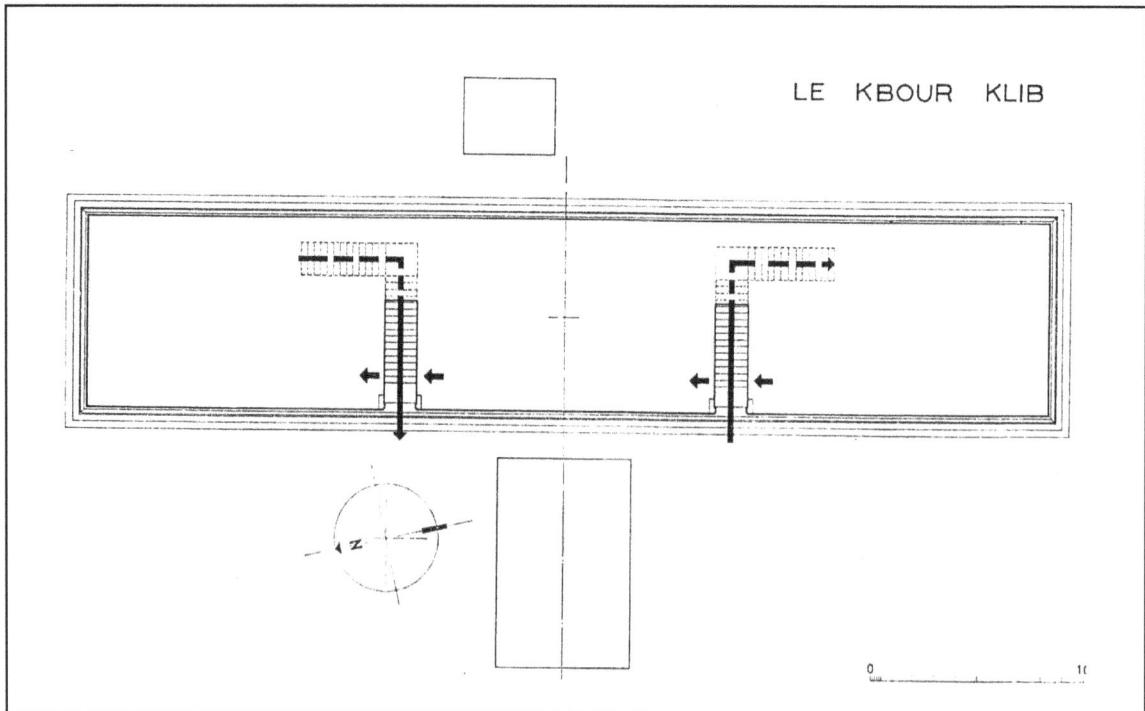

*Fig. 15. Proposed reconstruction of stairs to allow access
to the top of Kbor Klib. (Lézine 1968: Fig. 11)*

The environs of the Chemtou marble quarries, including the site of the ruined monument with decorations similar to those of Kbor Klib (*Fig. 17*), were the subjects of investigations by a German led team over the course of nearly 30 years commencing in the late 1960's. In 1979 Friedrich Rakob published initial results of these investigations in an article in *Die Numider*, a book accompanying a museum exhibition on the Numidian culture. In this publication Rakob dated the Chemtou monument to around 148 B.C., and suggested that it was a high sanctuary, constructed by the Numidian king Micipsa (148-118 B.C.), to honor his father, Massinissa

(1979b: 464). A proposed reconstruction of the monument was included (*Fig. 18*). Due to the decorative similarities between the two structures, the article described Kbor Klib. However, while the article speculated that Kbor Klib might also have been a "Monumentalaltar", it did not propose a chronology, noting that more investigation was required. The article included the Lézine reconstructions of Kbor Klib, photographs of some of the recovered elements, and, for the first time in any published article, a photograph of the monument (Rakob 1979a: 129-132).

In a 1980 article on Numidian architecture, Picard reviewed the work of Rakob on the monument at Chemtou, and related that work to the investigations of Kbor Klib. Picard noted that Rakob had considered that the Chemtou monument would have been surmounted by a second story. However, he believed that this postulated upper story was "très hypothétique", and was based on the same sort of supposition which had caused Lézine to propose a second story for Kbor Klib. Picard considered this reconstruction, at Kbor Klib at least, "entièrement gratuite", as the top of that monument had been destroyed. Picard also took exception to Lézine's interpretation of the Juba I coin which Lézine had used in support of his argument for a superstructure. Picard believed that this coin perhaps represented a basilica, and that in any case could not be used as a model for the original configuration of either Kbor Klib or Chemtou (Picard 1980: 16-19).

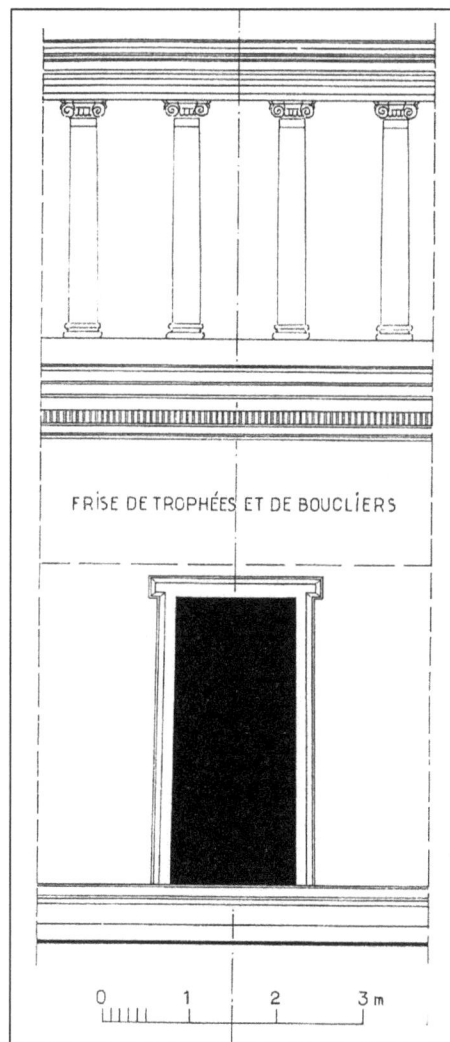

Fig. 16. Reconstruction of section of west façade. (Lézine 1968: Fig. 10)

15

Fig. 17. Shield and cuirass recovered at Chemtou.

In this article Picard finally did abandon the theory of Kbor Klib as a trophy to Caesar. Instead, he proposed that the interpretation most compatible with the data for both Kbor Klib and Chemtou would be as monuments "destinés à exalter la gloire divine et non les hauts faits des hommes" (1980: 17). While he accepted the close similarity in decoration between Kbor Klib and Chemtou, and noted that Chemtou had been securely dated to the mid-second century B.C., Picard in this article (apparently his last on the monument) did not address the chronology of Kbor Klib (1980: 16).

In an article on Numidian funerary architecture published in 1988, the authors Coarelli and Thébert mentioned both Kbor Klib and the monument at Chemtou. However, the two structures were noted only as examples of non-funerary Numidian architecture, and were described instead as sanctuaries (Coarelli & Thébert 1988: 764).

After a hiatus of 40 years, excavations were once again carried out at Kbor Klib during investigations directed by Naïdé Ferchiou. Published in 1991, hers was a thorough examination, thoroughly described and documented. It included sondages around the monument and a detailed description of the current state of the structure, as well as a meticulous examination of many of the artifacts recovered by Déroche and Prenat, still in the Bardo museum.

In one of several succinct observations, Ferchiou noted that due to its orientation "Kbor Klib tourne le dos" on Ksar Toual Zouameul. She further observed that the monument was masked by the topography when approached from the east, but was "visible du loin couronne encore majestueusement le sommet plat qui le porte" to those approaching from the west. (Ferchiou 1991: 45).

16

Ferchiou commenced her investigation with a description of the monument in its current state, noting the interior construction of roughly quarried and broken local stone, bound together with a native clay. She observed that the facing stones were carefully finished, and that the joints between these stones were "les plus beaux qu'on puisse voir en Proconsulaire." However, she remarked that the joints of the facing stones were not regular, presenting no particular rhythm, and that the interior courses did not line up with those of the facing. This arrangement she contrasted with the other known Hellenistic period monuments from the North African coast. Ferchiou also reported that lead had been used in certain locations to level the individual blocks.

Ferchiou included in her report a plan view of the current condition of Kbor Klib (*Fig. 19*), which differed little from the one prepared by Lézine 40 years earlier (*Fig. 12*, above). She also included, for the first time, an elevation of the existing condition of the monument viewed from the west.

Ferchiou included in her report a plan view of the current condition of Kbor Klib (*Fig. 19*), which differed little from the one prepared by Lézine 40 years earlier (*Fig. 12*, above). She also included, for the first time, an elevation of the existing condition of the monument viewed from the west.

Fig. 18. Chemtou monument proposed reconstruction model (Rakob 1979b: Tafel 40).

17

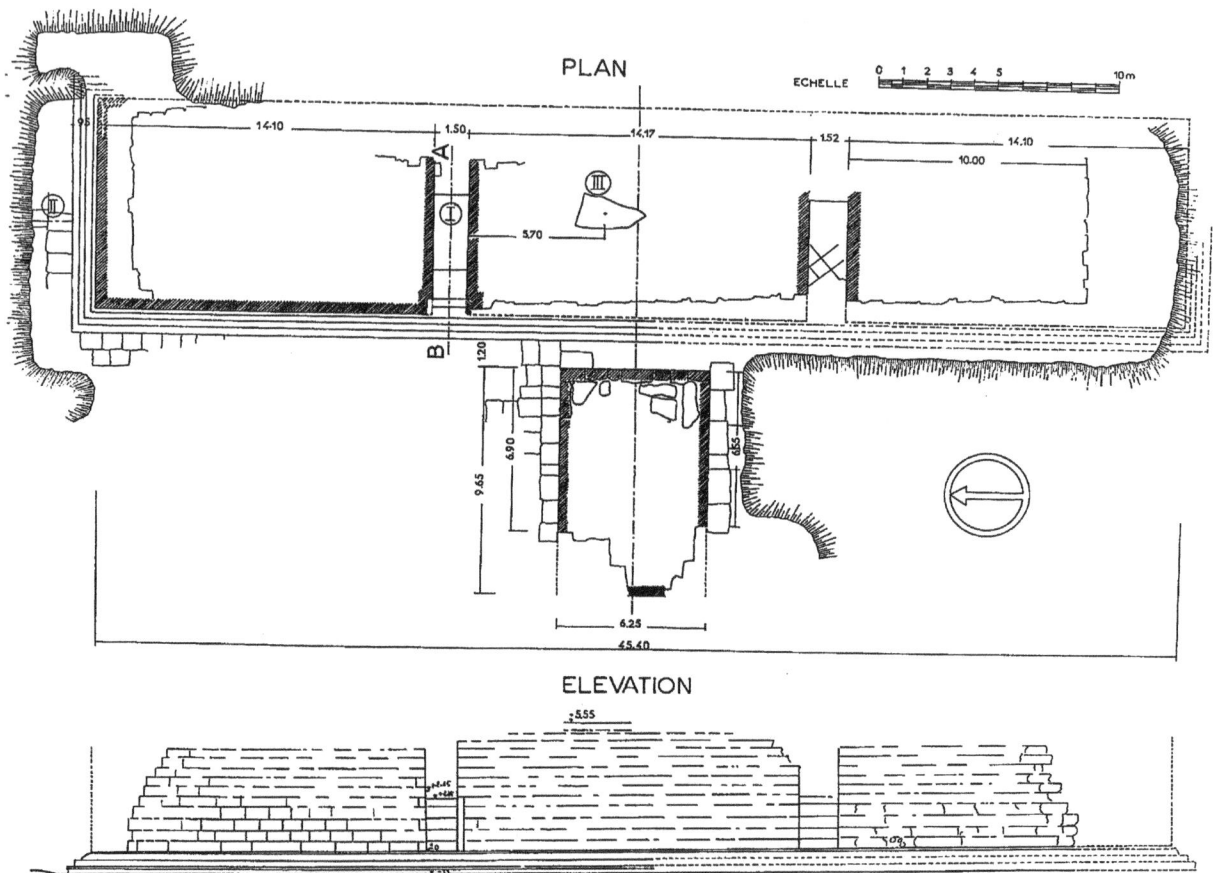

Fig. 19. Kbor Klib existing condition plan and elevation (Ferchiou 1991: Figg. 3-4).

Ferchiou then described some of the problems associated with any investigation of Kbor Klib, observing that no document gave any indication of its original configuration or purpose. She noted that the deteriorated condition of the monument, and of the architectural elements recovered from it, complicated any understanding of the original appearance. Further, she remarked that the original investigators had not been fastidious in documenting their finds, so that the locations where architectural fragments had been discovered were not known, thus complicating the task of determining their original positions.

Her sondages allowed Ferchiou to report on the construction of the foundations of Kbor Klib, and she noted the preparation of the subsurface soil, and the laying method of the bearing courses of stone. She then described what she considered to have been the original configuration of the monument above grade, consisting of a profiled base, a wall, a frieze of arms and a cornice. Ferchiou reported difficulty in determining whether the frieze would have run the entire length of the structure, as the widths of the recovered shield and cuirass (assuming these were alternated), did not divide neatly into the total length of the monument. She nonetheless thought a frieze running along the entire face of Kbor Klib more likely.

Ferchiou painstakingly described the architectural components discovered at Kbor Klib, including the columns, capitals, bases, cornices and the decorative elements constituting the presumed frieze of arms, apparently tracking them down in the storage magazines at the Bardo museum. For those elements where only fragments had been recovered, she recreated what she believed would have been the original configuration. She then evaluated the stylistic development of all of these components in the Mediterranean context, and proposed a chronology for the production of the assembly.

For the cuirasses from the frieze of arms, like Picard before her, Ferchiou noted similarities to breastplates known from the monument at Pergamon. The shields from the frieze, which she reported included the oval *thyreos* form (*Fig. 20*) in addition to the round form such as the one bearing the Artemis bust, she only dated to the Hellenistic period. The cornices from the monument she believed dated to at least the second century B.C., if not earlier, and bore similarities to cornices from Pergamon. For the column bases, and, more importantly, the capitals, she agreed with Lézine that they pre-dated the fall of Carthage, and in fact she noted features which for her were "indices en faveur d'une datation haute" (Ferchiou 1991: 89).

Ferchiou reconciled this stylistic chronological evidence with the admittedly meager ceramic material recovered during her excavations. She accepted the similarity between certain elements of the decorative schemes of Chemtou and Kbor Klib, and consequently considered the proposed chronology for Chemtou. The weight of this evidence suggested to her a mid-second century B.C. date for the construction of Kbor Klib, and the ancient Greek unit of measurement she believed was used on the monument allowed her to surmise a more precise date of "peu avant ou peu après le milieu du IIe s. av. J.C.". (Ferchiou 1991: 95).

Ferchiou examined the possible placement of many of these architectural elements, in particular the columns. Like Lézine, Ferchiou noted that fragments of two distinct types of column capitals had been collected at Kbor Klib. Picard had suggested that these belonged to a colonnade associated with the altar (Picard 1948: 422). Ferchiou argued against this location for the columns, having found no indication of bases there, and observed that columns rising from the altar would have obscured the frieze on the main monument (Ferchiou 1991: 68). Instead, she accepted Lézine's proposal of a colonnade on top of the main monument, and showed one in

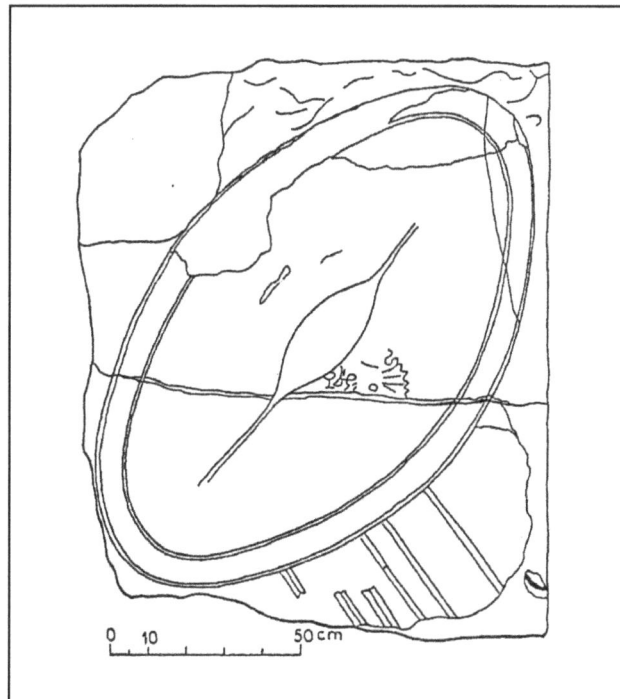

Fig. 20. Thyreos recovered from Kbor Klib (Ferchiou 1991: Fig. 22).

19

her hypothetical reconstruction of the west façade (*Fig. 21*). She also provided the first reconstruction of the frieze of arms (*Fig. 22*). The western façade, she believed, would have born the round shield forms and one of the two cuirass forms discovered. The lesser important east façade would have born the oval thyreos shields and the second cuirass form. In this she followed the reconstruction of Chemtou, where similar shield forms had been recovered, and had been tentatively assigned to the two sides of the monument, with the *thyreoi* decorating the less important western face (*Fig. 26*, below).

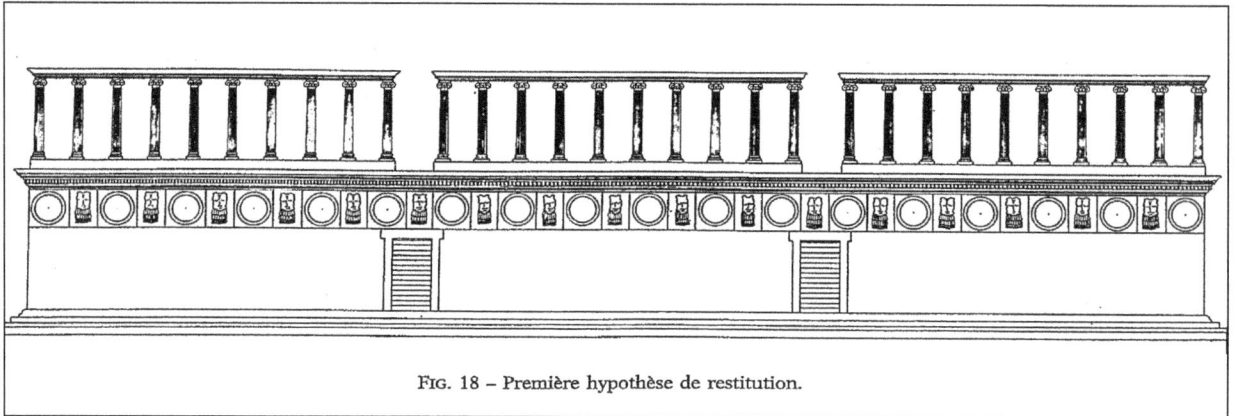

FIG. 18 – Première hypothèse de restitution.

Fig. 21. West façade proposed reconstruction with colonnade (Ferchiou 1991: Fig. 18).

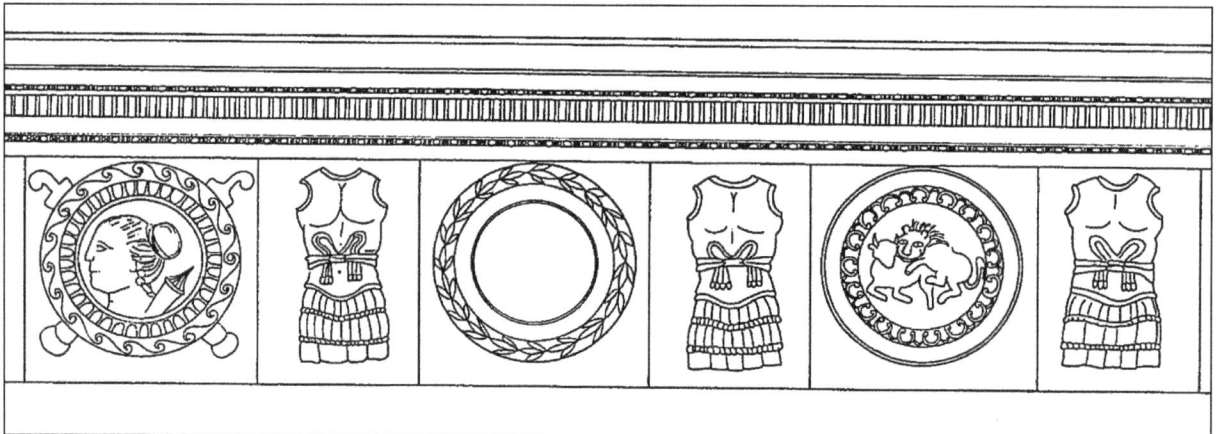

Fig. 22. Frieze of arms proposed reconstruction (Ferchiou 1991: Fig. 20).

Ultimately, Ferchiou argued that Kbor Klib represented something unique in Numidian, indeed Mediterranean, architecture. Kbor Klib diverged markedly from the construction and the ornamentation of all other known Numidian funerary structures. Neither did it resemble, in either configuration or style, known monuments or tombs from contemporary cultures, other than a resemblance, proposed by Ferchiou, to the *haouanet* burials of the Berber society. While certain elements of the decoration recalled those of the monument at Chemtou, there were fundamental differences. Kbor Klib is much larger than the monument at Chemtou. Chemtou consisted of a single rectangular structure, while Kbor Klib is composed of three rectangular stone masses on a single base. Chemtou bore Egyptian influenced decorations, and this influence is nowhere indicated in the worked stone artifacts recovered at Kbor Klib. Chemtou contained pilasters, not a feature of Kbor Klib. The architectural elements reflect that Chemtou was built to a Doric order, while Kbor Klib was Ionic. Kbor Klib therefore represented a significant departure from all other known classical structures. Despite the differences between

Chemtou and Kbor Klib, however, Ferchiou did conclude that both monuments must have been the product of a single, considered political agenda (Ferchiou 1991: 75 & 95-97).

Ferchiou's evaluation of the extant structure of Kbor Klib led her to an important observation regarding the stairs. The solution adopted by Lézine, with second flights turned at right angles to permit the stairs to reach the top of the monument, was impossible. The walls of the passages that contained the stairs continue basically through the monument without any sign of the widening that would be required to accommodate the second flight (*Fig. 15*, above). Therefore, the stairs were unlikely ever to have reached the top of the monument. (Ferchiou 1991: 60).

This observation led Ferchiou to surmise that the stairs went, if not to the summit, then to dual chambers within the body of the monument (*Fig. 23*). These chambers, she believed, would have been funerary, constructed to hold a burial. She therefore proposed that Kbor Klib might have been what it was originally perceived to be: a mausoleum. Ferchiou further suggested that there may have been chapels over these funeral chambers (*Fig. 23 & 24*), and that these could have been the location and configuration of the columns, with one type of capital over one of the chambers, and the second type over the other. She recognized how "choquant" this arrangement might be to classical norms, while arguing that it would not necessarily have been so to the members of the culture that built it (Ferchiou 1991: 60 & 68-70).

Concerning the location of Kbor Klib, Ferchiou observed that the monument is turned toward the west, and was therefore related to "une ville de la plaine du Sers, ou la plaine elle-même", and speculated that Zama Regia might have been located on the slopes dominated by Kbor Klib. She also suggested that the monument could have been associated with a territorial appropriation by the Numidian kingdom (Ferchiou 1991: 95-96).

Ferchiou's investigation of the smaller structure immediately to the west of Kbor Klib led her to conclude that it was contemporary with the main monument. She followed the lead of earlier investigators in referring to this smaller structure as an altar (Ferchiou 1991: 75-76). Ferchiou did not consider the remnants of a small structure to the east of the monument (fig. 12, above) to be significant (Ferchiou 1991: 45).

In 1994 the excavations at Chemtou were published in a two-volume work. During Rakob's evaluation of the monument there he once again discussed Kbor Klib. Kbor Klib, he believed, was somewhat later than his own monument, which he dated to the early 140's B.C. He entertained Ferchiou's suggestion that Kbor Klib was a mausoleum, but remained convinced that Chemtou was from the beginning a religious sanctuary, with no possible funerary function. This article included drawings of proposed reconstructions of both the east and west façades of the monument (figs. 25 & 26). The false door on the east façade reconstruction of Chemtou constituted for Rakob a cultic niche, as opposed to the real doors at Kbor Klib. His discussion of Kbor Klib was limited, and he did not offer his own opinion concerning its function or location (Rakob 1994: 34-35).

In a 1998 article entitled "Sobre la Identificacion de Dea Caelestis en Monumentos del Museo del Bardo (Tunez)" M. Paz Garcia-Bellido attempted to identify images associated with the goddess Caelestis on artifacts in the Bardo museum. As part of this exercise, she evaluated items recovered both from Kbor Klib and from Chemtou (although the Chemtou artifacts are not at the Bardo). She believed that the shield-born female figure shown on the reconstructions of both monuments actually represent Caelestis, instead of the Artemis usually identified. She therefore speculated that both monuments were dedicated to Caelestis. (Garcia-Bellido 1998: 5-6).

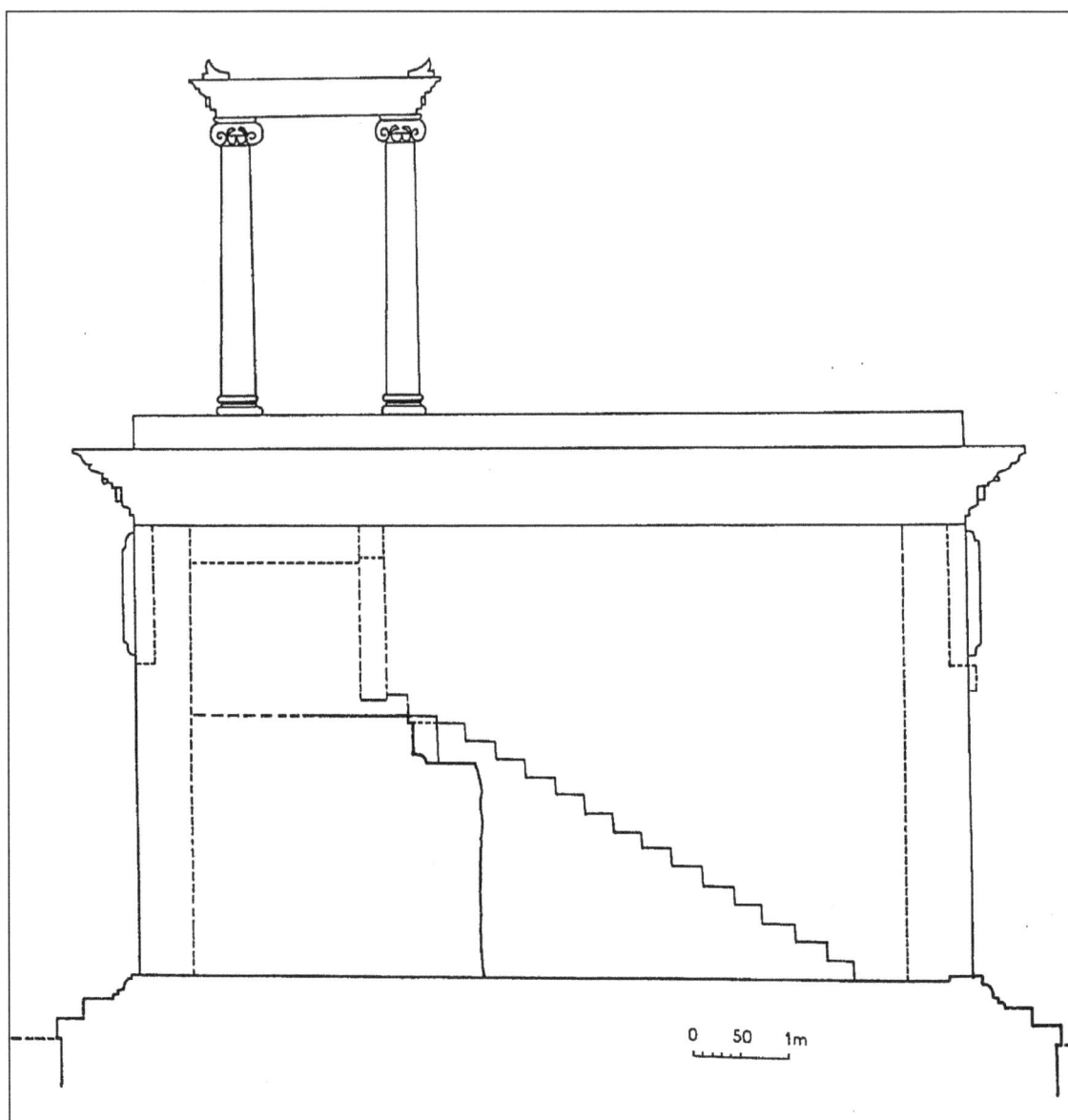

*Fig. 23. Proposed reconstruction of stair and funerary chamber,
with chapel above (Ferchiou 1991: Fig. 25).*

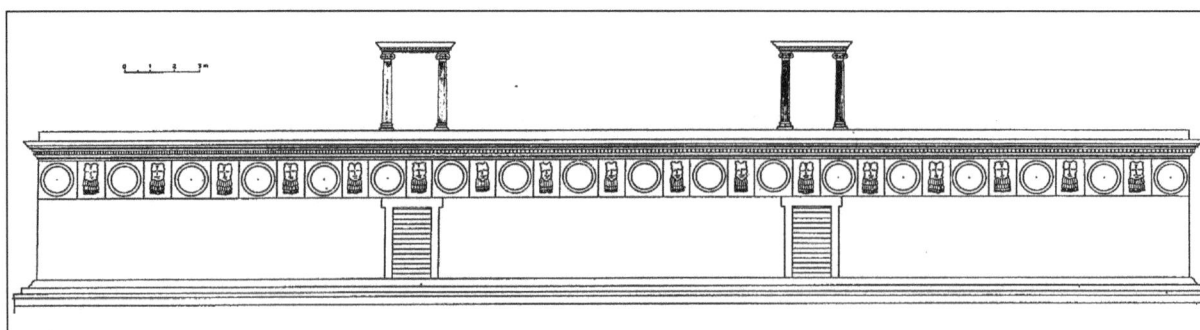

Fig. 24. West façade proposed reconstruction with chapels (Ferchiou 1991: Fig 19).

Fig. 25. Reconstruction of east façade of Chemtou monument (Rakob 1994: Abb. 7).

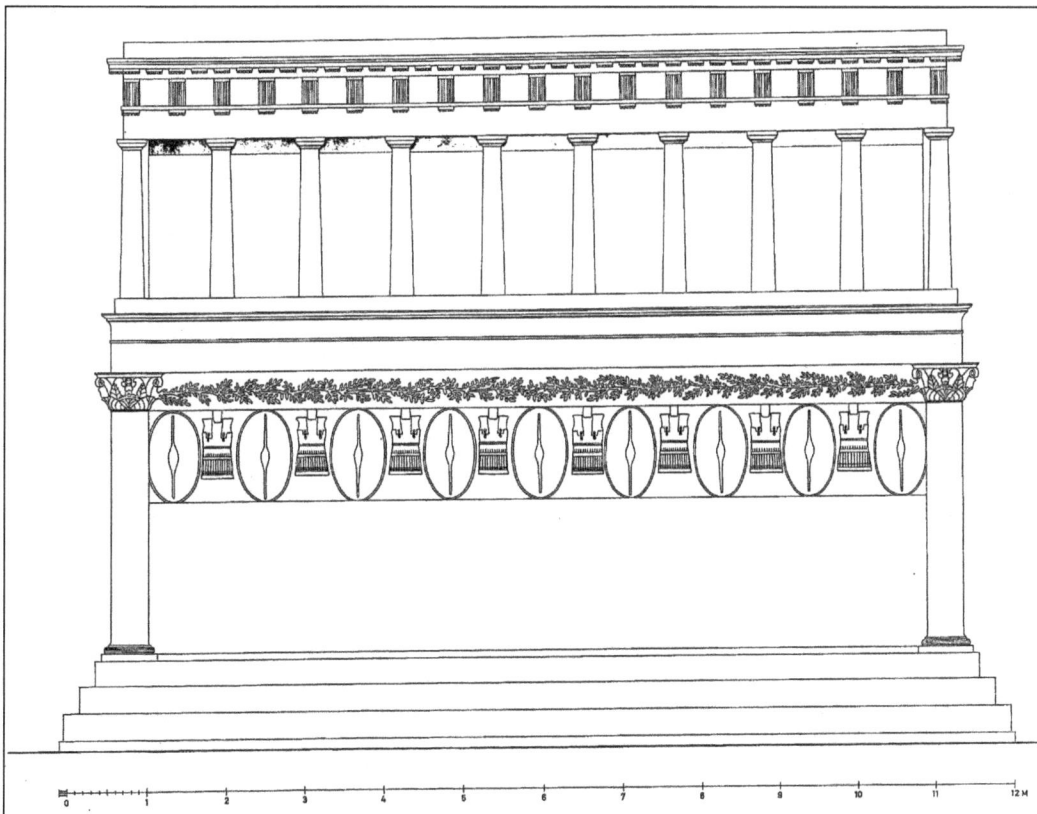

Fig. 26. Reconstruction of west façade of Chemtou monument (Rakob 1994: Abb. 10).

In a 1999 article entitled "Une Hypothèse sur une Série de Boucliers de Macédoine en Numidie" Eugenio Polito also evaluated the architectural elements recovered from Chemtou and Kbor Klib, as well as the investigations of those monuments by Rakob and Ferchiou. Polito proposed an association between both monuments and the involvement of the kingdom of Numidia as an ally of Rome in the second century B.C. wars between Rome and Macedonia, using to support this hypothesis iconographic details of the architectural decoration of those monuments which he believed were drawn from the Macedonian repertoire.

Polito started by revisiting the chronological conclusions of Rakob and Ferchiou, and accepted that Chemtou and Kbor Klib both dated from the mid-second century B.C. He argued that during this period decorative friezes of arms, which the monuments bore, would have had Macedonian antecedents (Polito 1999: 43). Polito then examined the architectural elements surviving from these friezes, identifying Macedonian characteristics, particularly in the form and decoration of the shields. He noted that there was a historical connection between the kingdom of Numidia and the ancient Macedonian kingdom which could explain this stylistic connection (Polito 1999: 47-48).

Polito reported that, according to the ancient sources, a son of the Numidian royal family had participated on the Roman side in the Second Macedonian War, been honored by the Roman Senate for his valor, and possibly died on the return voyage. He speculated that this prince might have been honored with a commemorative monument at Chemtou, one that included symbols glorifying his martial feats against the Macedonians. Alternately, Polito speculated that Chemtou originally had a purely religious function, still celebrating the Numidian contribution to the Roman victories over Macedonia, and that Kbor Klib might have entombed either the deceased prince, or other members of the Numidian royal family, also with some association to the Macedonian wars (Polito 1999: 64-65). As for the location of the monuments, Polito noted that Kbor Klib and the monument at Chemtou "dominaient respectivement les territoires des deux villes royales de Bulla et Zama" (Polito 1999: 39). Polito appears to have been the last to publish an investigation of Kbor Klib.

Summary

These investigations comprise the substantive research connected with Kbor Klib, and reflect the speculation concerning the chronology, function and location of the monument. After nearly 65 years of serious, if intermittent, consideration, opinions concerning Kbor Klib have in many respects converged.

Physically, the overall size and shape of Kbor Klib can still be seen. The monument is accepted to face west, and to have been decorated with a frieze of arms of alternating shields and cuirasses. Markings leave little doubt that there were at one time stairs in the passages, and other evidence confirms that the passages were closed with doors. The recovery of several column capital fragments confirms that freestanding columns were associated with the monument, even if there is disagreement regarding the location of these components. Investigators recognize the decorative similarities between Kbor Klib and Chemtou, as well as a Hellenistic influence for those decorations. The smaller structure to the west of Kbor Klib is considered an altar, contemporary with the main monument. There is uncertainty concerning some of the architectural details, particularly the cornice shapes, the locations of the columns, and the destination of the stairs. However, these questions seem tacitly accepted as subordinate to the issues of chronology and function.

Notwithstanding the consensus regarding the overall form of the monument, one observation that has escaped specific discussion in the published investigations of Kbor Klib is the relative heights of the individual sections that constitute the body of the monument. The archaeologist in charge of stabilization efforts currently ongoing at Kbor Klib, Professor Mansour Ghaki, suggests that the center section of the monument would have been higher in antiquity than the north and south sections (Ghaki 2004). This difference in height is still evident, with the center section taller by two courses of stone, or approximately 85 cm (figs. 6, above, & 27). The anomaly is in fact reflected in Ferchiou's elevation view of the west façade of the structure (fig. 19, above), but she does not refer to it in her written description, apparently believing that the height difference was attributable to the greater degradation of the north and south sections. Instead, Ferchiou's proposed recreations of the monument show one level of elevation across the top of the structure (*Figs. 21 & 24*). If the center section was higher in antiquity, neither of the proposed reconstructions, consisting of a second story composed of a colonnade running the length of the monument, or of chapels spanning between the sections, can be accurate.

Fig. 27. Top of Kbor Klib, looking south from north section,
showing the center section two courses higher.

Although Lézine's proposed reconstruction of Kbor Klib shows only a narrow portion of the monument (*Fig. 16*), his second story runs levelly across two sections. He, also, apparently attributed the difference in elevations between the sections to the greater deterioration of those on the north and south sides.

A difference in height between the sections of Kbor Klib would have implications for any frieze of arms, as well as for the second story. Ferchiou debated whether the frieze would have run the entire length of the façade of the monument, or been limited either to one side or the other, or to only the center section. Ultimately her solution was to show the frieze completely across the west face. Lézine also appeared to favor a continuous frieze along the west façade, as his reconstruction shows the feature across two sections of the monument. However, it is difficult to visualize a continuous frieze, as shown in both these reconstructions, across sections of differing heights. Thus for the frieze, as for the second story, although there is some degree of consensus among the investigators, a different solution is undoubtedly required if the center section was higher in antiquity.

Chronologically, there is consensus, with Picard's abandonment of a Caesarian connection, that Kbor Klib dates from the middle of the second century B.C. This consensus seems securely supported by the stylistic evaluation of the architectural components recovered at Kbor Klib in the context of the chronology of the development of these components. The column capitals and the cornices from the monument, in particular, seem to be firmly placed in the stylistic progression of these elements, through time, in the North African milieu. The style of the recovered armaments supports this dating, as do the (admittedly meager) ceramic finds. The archaic construction of the interior of the monument certainly would support this chronology. Despite the eastern Mediterranean decorative influences, the monument is attributed to the local Numidian culture, even if Greek craftsmen may have been imported for its execution.

Every investigator addressing the issue of location has suggested a connection between Kbor Klib and the Numidian city of Zama, even if there is disagreement concerning the nature of the connection. The isolated position of the monument, on a natural pass between the Plains of Siliana and of Sers has been remarked, as has the sweeping vista over the Plain of Sers.

Opinions diverge most significantly when it comes to function. Chronology dictated abandonment of the hypothesis that Kbor Klib was constructed by or to honor the deeds of Julius Caesar, although the possibility that it represented some sort of monumental trophy was not therefore eliminated. It is worth noting that the size, setting and unique character of the structure convinced the earlier researchers that they were in the presence of a truly important monument, which could only be explained by some connection with Caesar. The most recent investigators are willing to accept Ferchiou's proposal of a funerary character, without abandoning the possibility that it could also commemorate a military event (as she herself suggested). While no investigator disputes some religious connotation, two have suggested that Kbor Klib was strictly a religious monument. Whatever its function, Kbor Klib is agreed to have been the product of the Numidian kingdom of the second century B.C., and it is there we must look to determine the political circumstances surrounding its construction.

Chapter 2
The Second Century B.C. North African Political Landscape

Before the second century B.C., the term Numidia had no relevance in the context of a North African political entity. The dominant regional power was the city-state of Carthage, which gradually became so following its foundation in the eighth or ninth century B.C. By 310 B.C., Carthage exercised direct control over what is now northern Tunisia, and by the end of the third century ruled "much of Tunisia and eastern Algeria" (Brett & Fentress 1996: 24).

During this same period, the semi-nomadic Berber populations of the areas surrounding the zone of Carthaginian control were coalescing into states, one supposition holding that the act of state formation was in reaction to the expanding Carthaginian power. By the end of the third century B.C., two kingdoms, the Massyli and the Masaesyli, occupied the region that became Numidia. The Massyli were the immediate neighbors of Carthage, abutting Carthaginian territory on the west, south and (possibly) the east. The kingdom of the Masaesyli bordered the Massyli to the west, extending along the North African coastline through much of what is now northern Algeria (*Fig. 28*). While there was still no country known as Numidia, at this time the Carthaginians began to refer to the peoples outside their immediate zone of control as Numidians (Brett & Fentress 1996: 24-25).

Fig. 28. Map of North Africa showing pre-Numidian kingdoms.
(available on line at: http://www.barca.fsnet.co.uk/Graphics/map-north-africa.gif)

The rise of the Roman state as a Mediterranean power, and the consequent friction with Carthage, placed the North African kingdoms in an influential, and dangerous, position, as allies or opponents of one or the other of these contending entities. In fact, it is with this competition, and the resultant Roman interest in North African affairs, that the Numidian predecessor kingdoms enter the surviving written record. Roman historians recorded the struggle for primacy between Rome and Carthage, and some of those accounts survive.

There is not much record of Numidian involvement during the First Punic War between Rome and Carthage (264-241 B.C.), although they likely provided cavalry, for which they were famous, to the Carthaginians (Goldsworthy 2000: 32, 65-128). However, contemporaneous with their war with Rome, Carthage attempted increasing the African territory under her direct control at the expense of the neighboring kingdoms, with ensuing bitter fighting around 256

B.C. (Goldsworthy 2000: 87). It is unclear what were the results of this conflict, but it seems representative of the changeable nature of the relationship between Carthage and her North African neighbors.

Relatively thorough accounts do exist for Numidian involvement in the Second Punic War (218-201 B.C.). At the outbreak of this War, the kingdom of the Massyli was ruled by Gaia, while that of the Masaesyli was ruled by Syphax. For the first five years of the conflict Gaia opposed the Carthaginians, while Syphax was allied with them. In 213 B.C. Syphax broke with Carthage, which thereupon made alliance with Gaia. For the next six years the young son of Gaia, Massinissa, served the Carthaginian interests, leading Numidian cavalry in actions against the Masaesylian forces in North Africa, and against the Romans in Spain in 212-211 B.C., and again in 208-207 B.C. (Walsh 1965: 150).

By 206 B.C., however, a number of critical circumstances had changed, particularly for Massinissa. Most importantly, his father Gaia was dead, and the Massyli kingdom was in the hands of a regent inimical to Massinissa and operating against his interests both with Carthage and with Syphax (Walsh 1965:150). Syphax had become reconciled with Carthage (Brett & Fentress 1996: 26). In addition, the Romans, for so long the potential loser in the lengthy struggle, were now resurgent. Under these circumstances, Massinissa approached the Romans in Spain about the possibility of an alliance. He then departed for Africa and his own affairs. During the next two years Massinissa was unable to supplant the adversary ruling his father's former kingdom. Instead, he ultimately became a fugitive, and was lucky to escape capture or death (Walsh 1965: 150). Perhaps his misfortunes were lightened by the knowledge that the Romans, too, were coming to Africa.

In 204 B.C. the Italian theatre of the Second Punic War was effectively stalemated, with Hannibal contained in the southern part of the peninsula and the Romans avoiding a direct engagement. In Spain, however, the Roman general Scipio had defeated the Carthaginian forces. In an effort to force a conclusion to the war, he now invaded the Carthaginian heartland. Massinissa was waiting for him.

Joining the Romans upon their landing in Africa with a force of only 200 cavalry, Massinissa immediately proved his value during engagements with the Carthaginians. Victory during these encounters improved the fortunes of the Romans, and so too improved the fortunes of Massinissa. Eventually, Scipio provided Massinissa with sufficient Roman forces for him to regain his father's kingdom, capture his rival Syphax, and begin to conquer the kingdom of the Masaesyli (Walsh 1965: 150-151).

Massinissa was occupied in this last endeavor when recalled by Scipio in time to join the Roman army for the deciding engagement of the Second Punic War, the battle of Zama. During the engagement Massinissa's cavalry, returning from pursuit of the fleeing enemy horse, fell on the rear of the Hannibal's forces and decided the battle (Polybius: 15.5-14). The defeated Carthaginians were forced to make peace on Roman terms.

The treaty of 201 B.C. ending the war between Carthage and Rome stipulated that Carthage was to return to Massinissa his ancestral lands, without defining what those lands were. Additionally, the Romans conferred honors and titles on Massinissa, and awarded him the territories they had captured from his rival Syphax (Walsh 1965: 151-156). The onetime fugitive, disowned prince was suddenly a power in North Africa.

Once the Romans departed, having under the treaty greatly restricted the Carthaginian ability to wage war, and having levied a huge indemnity on the defeated city, Massinissa was able to exercise this power. One of the priorities of the Numidian ruler was territorial expansion. In addition to consolidating his hold on the former Masaesylian kingdom, Massinissa sought gains at the expense of Carthage. While the locations and chronology of Numidian seizures of Carthaginian territory are not universally agreed, *Fig. 30* is representative of the pattern by which Massinissa's kingdom increased in size during his rule. It was during the earlier part of Massinissa's reign that the name Numidia supplanted the names of the predecessor kingdoms. At the end of it, Numidia was territorially significant.

Carthage responded to these territorial predations with appeals to Rome for arbitration, in accordance with the 201 B.C. treaty. While initially somewhat sympathetic to the complaints of its former enemy, Rome in all cases but one refused to rule against its Numidian ally (Yates: 4). Nor was Massinissa passive during these exchanges, defending his own actions and, further, accusing Carthage of contravening the treaty in other regards. Eventually Rome displayed open partiality toward Massinissa in these territorial disputes. Carthage ultimately decided to resist with force the aggression of Massinissa, resulting in war between the two kingdoms, and the sending of a Carthaginian army against the Numidians in 150 B.C. The Numidians defeated this army, but the military action by Carthage, without the prior consent of Rome, constituted a breach of the 201 B.C. treaty. Rome used this breach as the excuse to commence the Third Punic War (149-146 B.C.), which resulted in the eradication of Carthage (Walsh 1965: 157-160).

Of the surviving ancient sources on the events surrounding the formation of Numidia the Greco-Roman historian Polybius is the one writing nearest in time, and the one considered most accurate. As he accompanied the Roman army during the Third Punic War, and was a friend of the Roman commander, Scipio (adoptive grandson of the victor of Zama), he is regarded as the historian with the best access to first hand information surrounding those events. Nonetheless Polybius is not considered infallible, as when he credits Massinissa with the introduction of agriculture to Numidia. The available evidence confirms that agriculture was practiced long before his rule (Walsh 1965: 152). Despite the exaggeration, Massinissa's reign did see some increase in the agricultural productivity of Numidia, reflected in grain surpluses from which he was able to make food contributions to Rome, principally in support of their military endeavors, and religious donations to the island of Delos. Massinissa is credited with the introduction into Numidia of vine and olive cultivation, the latter having regional impact still felt today, even if at the time the traditional stock-rearing pattern of life of the Numidians is not considered to have been seriously affected (Walsh 1965: 154).

Fig. 29. Bust of Hannibal, finally defeated with the aid of Numidian forces.

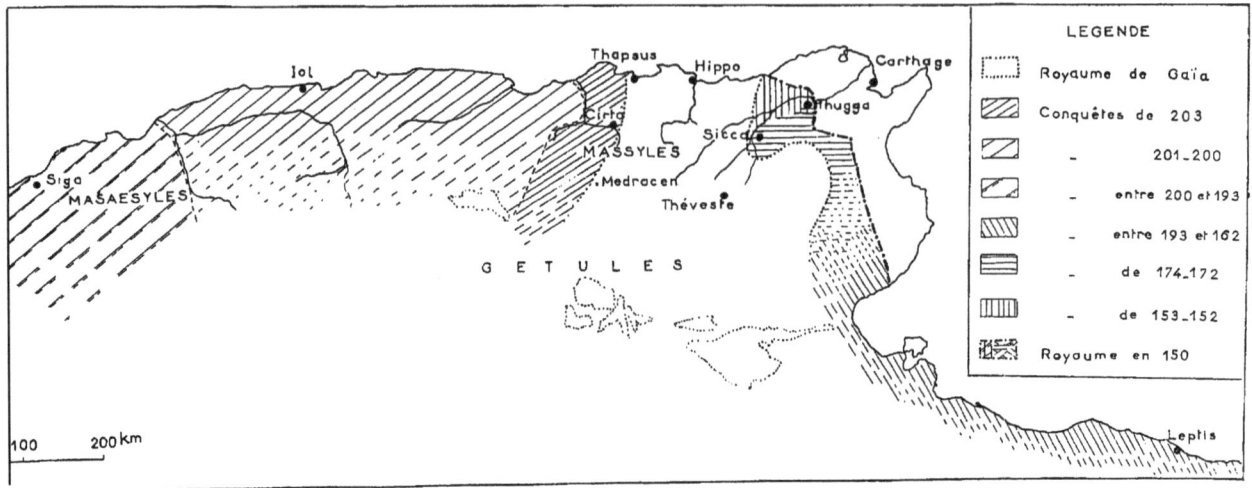

*Fig. 30. Map of Numidian territorial acquisitions during Massinissa's reign.
(Camps 1960: Fig. 18)*

In the area of trade it also does not appear that there were extreme increases during Massinissa's reign. Exports would have included wild animals for the increasing Roman appetite for games, some scale of luxury products including ivory and citrus wood, as well as agricultural surpluses and perhaps by-products of stock rearing. Luxury items for the nobility, and arms for the military would have been imported to some degree. However, no evidence apparently exists to support a burgeoning Numidian role in Mediterranean trade (Walsh 1965: 155).

Indeed, according to Brett & Fentress, "the Numidian landscape continued to be one of villages, practicing mixed farming and paying tribute in kind" (1996: 33). Nevertheless, the Numidian royal family became wealthy through collection of this tribute, as well as through indemnities imposed on appropriated Carthaginian settlements, and compensation extracted directly from Carthage as the result of Roman arbitration (Walsh 1965: 155)

Numidian coinage was produced, but only in base metals, with no gold or silver issues under Massinissa or his descendants. Imports were consequently "paid for by barter or foreign currency" (Walsh 1965: 155). There was thus no widespread economic flourishing, and whatever processes of economic improvement were ongoing in the society in general were apparently gradual.

Nor do there seem to have been systemic innovations in the way Massinissa administered his kingdom. All power remained concentrated in the royal house, including finance, diplomacy, justice and military affairs. Massinissa governed, according to Walsh, "utilizing the techniques of a Hellenistic king to impress his subjects", such as portraying himself on Numidian coinage (1965: 155). Picard has Massinissa spending all his life in overcoming the fickle tribal mentality of his subjects by establishing and enforcing the systems that would stabilize the population and legitimize his sole rule (1967: 242).

This process of legitimization and stabilization included something of a building program. Massinissa constructed a new palace at Cirta (Raven 1984: 47). His funerary monument, generally held to be the massive structure the *Medracen* (*Fig. 32*), bears eastern Mediterranean motifs and was probably created by Greek craftsmen (Coarelli & Thébert 1988: 765, Brett & Fentress 1996: 28-29). A series of unique tower tombs constructed for Numidian royalty (*Fig. 33*) "seems to have first appeared in Africa in the context of Numidian state-building" (Quinn 2003: 21), and Brett and Fentress agree that "...the tower tombs seem to have become one of the major symbols of nobility within the Numidian and Libyan heartlands" (1996: 31). Thus the stamp of the regime took the form of monuments reflecting its power and reach.

In the field of foreign policy Massinissa was "recognized as one of their own by other Hellenistic rulers". Statues of him were erected at Delos, his coinage followed the Hellenistic tradition, and Numidia was represented at the Panathenaean games (Brett & Fentress 1996: 27). Nonetheless, his principal foreign relations were with Carthage, and with Rome.

With Carthage, there must have been ambivalence. On the one hand there was serious (if intermittent) friction over territory, eventually leading to war. On the other, Appian advises that Massinissa was educated at Carthage (Appian: Chapter II, 10). He married at least one of his daughters into the Carthaginian elite, and his own grandson may have been in charge of the city during the Third Punic War (Yates: 3).

Fig. 31. Portrait of Massinissa, adapted from coin images believed to represent him. (available on line at: http://www.barca.fsnet.co.uk/masinissa.htm)

Fig. 32. The Medracen, Massinissa's putative tomb, Algeria: (available on line at: http://www.visit-algeria.com, © Mostefa BRAHIM/Agence Orianis)

Fig. 33. Examples of North African tower tombs. (Rakob 1979a: Abb. 104)

To Rome, Massinissa was a lifelong loyal client. His support for the Romans during their own conflicts included more than just the provision of grain. In 198 B.C. he sent 1,000 cavalry and 10 elephants in support of Roman actions against King Philip of Macedonia, and in 191 another 500 cavalry and 20 elephants were contributed against Antiochus. As noted above (Camps 1960: 227). As noted above, in 171 B.C. one of Massinissa's own sons led Numidian forces on the Roman side in the Third Macedonian War (Walsh 1965: 158-159). Assistance was also periodically rendered the Romans in Spain, and in 154 B.C. Massinissa himself, at the age of 84, participated in support of Roman action against rebellious tribes there (Yates: 3).

Thus throughout his reign Massinissa never forgot his allegiance to, and dependence upon, Rome. If he initially resented the arrival of the invading Roman army at the start of the Third Punic War, he nevertheless eventually offered assistance. He died in 148 B.C., before that assistance could be provided, but the offer was honored by his successors, one of his sons fighting with the Romans (Walsh 165: 160).

Numidia under Massinissa was culturally influenced by the eastern Mediterranean, with two of his sons being Greek scholars, one of these additionally a student of philosophy and the other a chariot racer at the Panathenaean games (Walsh 1965: 155). While the Numidian kingdom was embracing these foreign influences on the one hand, on the other old traditions held sway, even if these old traditions were themselves adopted from another culture. The language used at court was Punic, as were religious practices (Brett & Fentress 1996: 27). Nonetheless, the elites clearly aspired to legitimacy within the context of the Hellenistic states, in particular choosing "architectural decoration that celebrated the pervasive Greek and eastern Mediterranean influence in this period on all of Africa" (Quinn 2003: 21).

In the question of his succession Massinissa demonstrated true originality. Unable to decide which of three of his sons was best suited to succeed him, he requested the assistance of the younger Scipio in determining how to "assign the appropriate functions to each" of the three. Upon his death, although the kingdom itself remained whole, authority was divided, with one son in charge of the government, one bearing military responsibility and the third administering justice (Appian 105-107). By 138 B.C. two of these co-rulers had disappeared, and there was again but one king in Numidia, Micipsa, who ruled for another 20 years.

Micipsa seems to have concentrated on consolidating the hold of the Numidian royal house on the territory left by his father; at least the sources do not paint him as a particularly acquisitive ruler. Rome created a new province in Africa after the destruction of Carthage, making Rome and Numidia neighbors after 146 B.C. It is unlikely that Rome would have regarded benevolently an expansionist Numidian policy.

However, under Micipsa, Numidia continued to provide military support to Roman efforts (Yates: 4). The Hellenizing influences would have continued, and presumably there was an increased concentration of wealth and power among the elites, following the pattern under Massinissa. In another imitation of that pattern, when it came time for Micipsa to bequeath his kingdom he acted upon the advice of yet another member of the Scipio family, and in 118 B.C. authority was once again divided between three sons of the king (Brett & Fentress 1996: 41-42).

Summary

To speak of Numidia of the mid-second century B.C. in any political sense is in fact to speak of the kings Massinissa and Micipsa, and their families, and the elites that served them. And here we see wealth, and absolute power within their own domain. Initially at least we see territorial ambition, the drive for the land that bestowed wealth and power. We see a desire for recognition among the other Mediterranean kingdoms and for the legitimacy and status this recognition would provide. We see friction with Carthage, perhaps driven merely by territorial self-interest, but perhaps driven by a deeper resentment. Above all, we see a ruling class that must have calculated every significant action in consideration of the attitude, and possible reaction, of Rome.

The surviving accounts describing Numidia in the second century B.C. were written by the Romans. Even after correcting for this imbalance, it is difficult to overemphasize the influence of Rome on Numidia. Massinissa owed his kingdom to the Romans. Territorial increases were accomplished with their tacit approval or encouragement. Much of what trade there was would have been with Rome. Numidian resources, including a son of the king, were expended to serve Roman interests abroad. Upon the death of her kings, the fate of the kingdom was decided in consultation with Rome. Numidia assisted Rome during the brutal destruction of Carthage. Shortly after that event, Rome and Numidia were neighbors. And near the end of the Roman civil war the kingdom was effectively assimilated into the empire. From its creation until its demise, Numidia lived in the shadow of Rome.

No record has been found to explain why Kbor Klib was built, and why built where it was (Ferchiou 1991: 49). For these explanations, we are left with the speculation of the investigators. In consideration of the situation of the Numidia of the time, however, it is difficult to believe that, for a monument as imposing as this, there was no connection to the influence of Rome.

Chapter 3
Proposed Function and Meaning

Tomb Fit for Royalty

The word Kbor is a rough transliteration of the Arabic word for tomb, giving a funerary designation for Kbor Klib the merit of antiquity. However, earlier investigators dismissed this interpretation of the structure, due initially to the discovery of the architectural elements bearing martial decorations. As an understanding of the original configuration of the monument developed, the rejection of a funerary function strengthened. To quote Picard, "L'ordonnance générale diffère absolument de celle des tombeaux connus, qu'ils soient africains de toute époque, ou qu'ils appartiennent à une autre région méditerranéenne" (Picard 1948: 422). For Numidia in particular, the "tumulus" tomb and the tower tomb forms are well identified (*Fig. 32 & 33*), while mausoleums resembling Kbor Klib are unknown. In his seminal 1961 work on Numidian mortuary practices, and specifically his study of Berber grand mausoleums, Camps mentions neither Kbor Klib nor Chemtou (Camps 1961: 199-205). The only notice these structures receive in the 1988 Coarelli & Thébert study of the same subject is as examples of non-funerary Numidian architecture. Thus these investigators have discovered no stylistic similarities to known mausoleums warranting a funerary identification for Kbor Klib. When it comes to elite mausoleums during this period, Numidian royalty and nobility employed the tower tomb (*Fig. 34*) as a funerary monument "right across North Africa" (Brett & Fentress 1996: 29-31). A mortuary identification for Kbor Klib becomes even more questionable in light of the identification by Rakob of the only stylistically similar structure, at Chemtou, as a high sanctuary.

Fig. 34. Example of tower tomb, at Dougga, Tunisia.

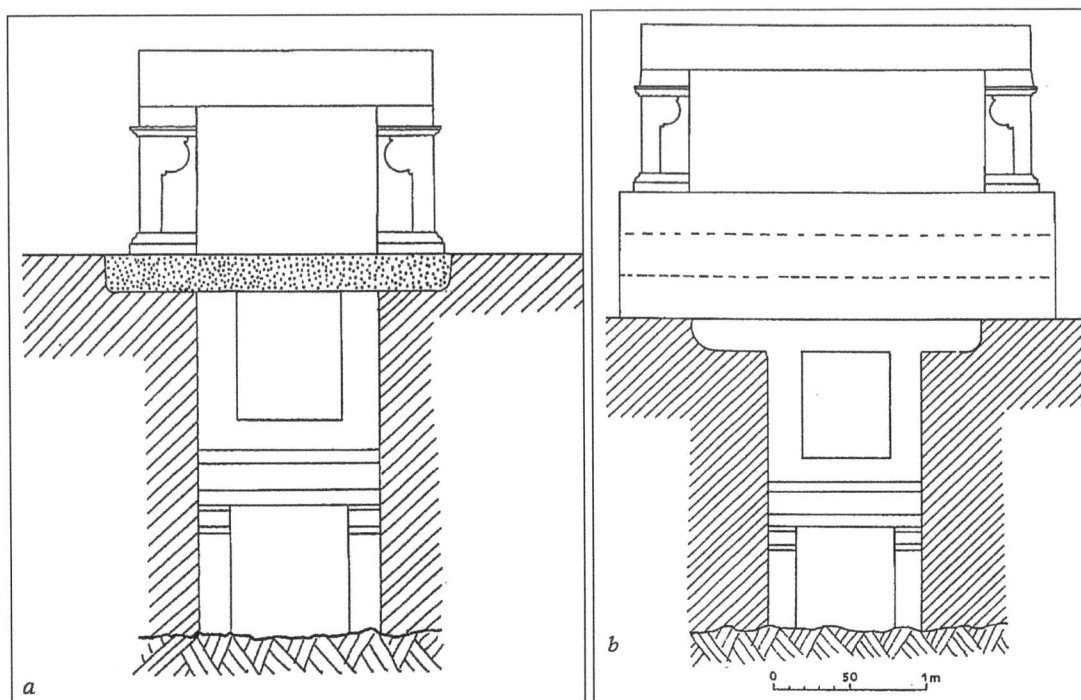

Figs. 35a & 35b. Haouanet reconstructions, with rock carved
burial chambers surmounted by above ground structures.
(Ferchiou 1991: Figs. 40a & 40b)

Nonetheless, in an ingenious solution to the problem of the destination of the stairs, Ferchiou hypothesized burial chambers within Kbor Klib, and returned to the identification of the monument as a mausoleum. In support of this attribution, she suggested a similarity of construction between Kbor Klib and certain *haouanet*, which are ancient rock-carved North African burial chambers. However, the arguments used to support this comparison are, to quote Polito, "assez vagues" (1999: 42), and it is difficult to accept the relationship between the *haouanet* illustrated in the Ferchiou article, with their underground burial chambers(*Fig. 35*), and the free-standing, classically decorated Kbor Klib.

Ferchiou stated, "Une autre argument en faveur d'une destination funéraire est l'orientation même des couloirs, qui regardent vers l'Occident; le Soleil couchant n'est-il pas justement un accompangnateur privilégié de l'âme des morts dans leur voyage pour l'au-delà?" (Ferchiou 1991: 61). And yet, in their 1998 survey of the orientations of the burial monuments of the pre-Roman cultures of Tunisia, Belmonte, Estaban and Gonzalez investigated three of the twelve known groups of *hawanat* and reported that, while burial chamber orientations ranged from 0° to 230° azimuth, there were a preponderance looking southeast, and not one between 230° and 315° azimuth. In other words, no *haouanet* were oriented toward the west (Belmonte 1998: S7, S12 & S13). It therefore seems that indigenous traditions of tomb orientation would argue against a funerary identification for Kbor Klib, considering its accepted facing direction.

After noting that Kbor Klib faced west, Ferchiou observed, "L'autel est, par contre, tourné vers l'est" (Ferchiou 1991: 61). However, Picard reported that the structure to the west of the main monument was "précédé vers l'Est par un escalier d'accès" (Picard 1957: 210). The remaining stonework on the east side of the altar does in fact suggest that steps at one time reached the top from that side (*Figs. 36 & 8*, above). Stairs on the east would indicate that the altar faced west, not east.

36

Fig. 36. East side of altar to west of Kbor Klib, showing possible stairs access to top of structure.

The proximity of the altar to the main monument, a distance of merely two meters, also indicates that the altar faced west (*Fig. 11,*). A representation of a priest officiating in front of another religious structure (*Fig. 37*) reflects the awkwardness of a similar exercise at Kbor Klib, where the altar was only some two meters high, in contrast to the six-meter high monument (Ferchiou 1991: 75). Turned toward the east a priest would be staring straight at the wall between the two doors of the monument, or officiating with his head thrown sharply back to see the top of the monument (*fig. 38*). Proximity, as well as the access stairs, supports a western orientation for the altar.

The existence of the altar, and its orientation, are important points. In his book on Numidian funerary structures Camps includes a picture of a mausoleum and notes an associated altar (Camps 1961: Plate IX). However, no mention is made of this feature in the text, and it seems that Numidian mausoleums did not characteristically possess altars. Camps did observe that a funeral monument is "un sanctuaire auprès duquel l'homme a toujours accompli des gestes d'offrande et de vénération" (1961: 173). This suggests that the ceremonial focus would be the monument itself, where the venerated individual rested. If there were to be an altar associated with a funerary monument, it would therefore be faced toward the monument. Such is not the case at Kbor Klib, where the construction strongly suggests that the altar faced away from the monument. A western orientation for the altar, combined with the more highly decorated west face of the main monument, would argue that the two structures gathered significance from that direction.

The stairs of Kbor Klib, which Ferchiou believed led to burial chambers within the monument, are themselves a curious feature. In the Ferchiou reconstruction these stairs lead to a wall closing off the crypt (*Fig. 22*). There is no landing in front of this wall, no place for any

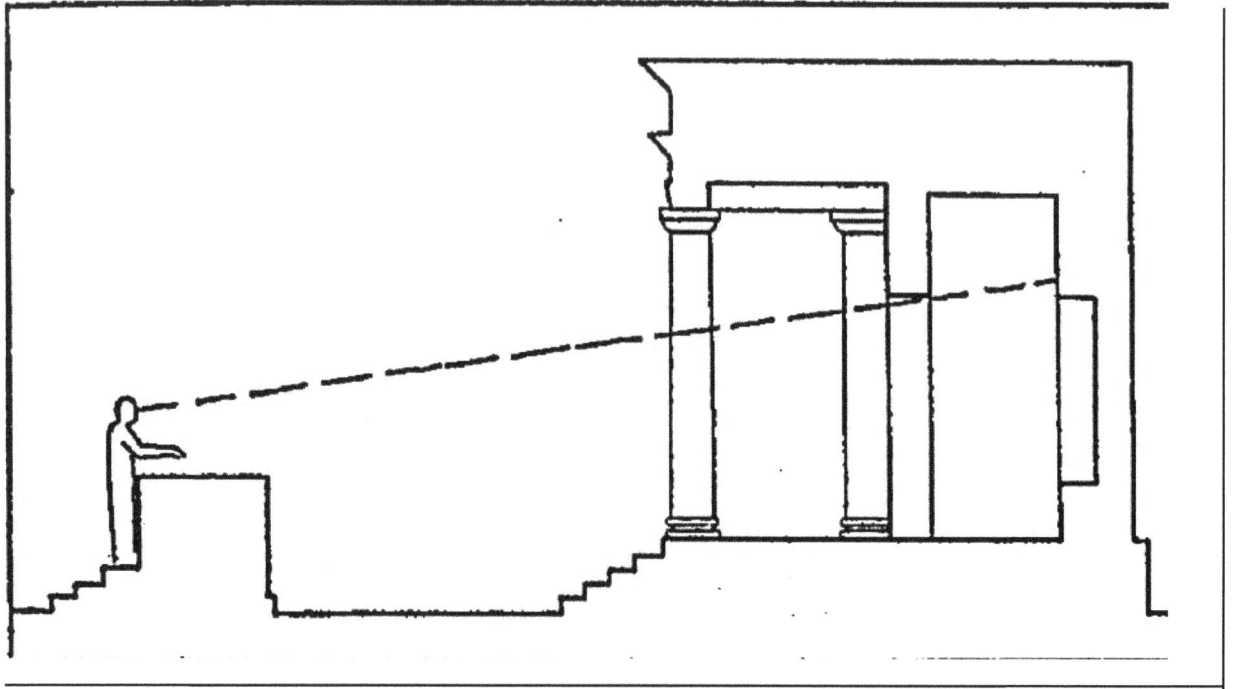

Fig. 37. Priest officiating at temple. Note distance from altar to votive niche.
(Lézine 1962: Fig. 16)

Fig. 38. Re-enactment of similar exercise at Kbor Klib.
Note proximity of monument to "altar".

ceremony, or for offerings. The stairs therefore serve no purpose. Ferchiou herself recognized that the stairs represented something of an anomaly, speculating, "Peut-être d'ailleurs, ces escaliers étaient-ils destinés à être démolis après l'ensevelissement des grands personnages auxquels le Kbor Klib était destiné" (Ferchiou 1991: 61). However, even this solution is unsatisfactory. Ramps would have made more sense as temporary constructions to facilitate moving sarcophagi into the chambers, and there would be no need of doors. For the stairways were at one time closed with doors, 3.2 meters high in Ferchiou's estimation (Ferchiou 1991: 52). These were narrow. The passages measure 1.5 meters wide, and the doors included large jambs inside the passages (Picard 1957: 209). The doors therefore can have been only a little over a meter wide. Thus we have stairs that really lead nowhere, accessed through monumentally high, narrow doors, which were obviously permanent features. This seems a curious configuration for a mausoleum.

Ferchiou calculated that the interior chambers were 1.5 meters wide, 1.8 meters deep and two meters high. In support of a funerary function for the chambers she compared this size favorably to a funerary vault at another Roman site in Tunisia, which was two meters in length, .99 meters in breadth and 1.545 meters in height. She also noted that *haouanet* chambers were often of similar proportions (Ferchiou 1991: 60). The antecedents of the Roman funerary vault are not given, but the *haouanet* at least are not royal burials, as even Ferchiou considered must be the case for Kbor Klib. A length of 1.8 meters seems insufficient for a royal sarcophagus, and in Ferchiou's reconstruction, with a panel closing off the chamber, the length is reduced to just over 1.5 meters. In other royal mausoleums the burial chambers are either fully accessible, with room around the sarcophagus for ceremonies of veneration (or additional family member internments), or they are completely inaccessible, walled up within the monument. It is possible that any interments at Kbor Klib were cremations rather than inhumations.[1] Even with only cremation urns centered in the spaces, however, and leaving out the wall at the top of the stairs shown in the Ferchiou reconstruction, the tiny chambers of Kbor Klib seem insufficiently large for any purpose. Yet doors and stairs were constructed to facilitate access to them.

The possible height difference between the sections of Kbor Klib, mentioned above, also raises questions about funeral chambers within the monument. Certainly Ferchiou's proposal of individual chapels surmounting each of the burial chambers, spanning between the sections of the monument (fig. 24, above), would be untenable.

Ferchiou declined to speculate whom Kbor Klib might have been designed to inter, simply observing that its construction can only have been "l'œuvre d'un prince" (Ferchiou 1991: 95). As noted above, Polito examined in some detail which members of the Numidian royal family might have been buried at Kbor Klib, suggesting several princes as candidates, but without deciding which of those would be most likely. Regardless of the individuals involved, however, it seems highly unusual for a royal mausoleum to be constructed for two equal internments, as would have been the case at Kbor Klib. Size and complexity argue that Kbor Klib was constructed, or at least designed, during the lives of the intended occupants. Hence we would have two members of the royal family deciding (or one deciding for both) that they will rest for eternity in different chambers, with equal status. Such a circumstance is perhaps more exceptional than the monument itself.

Thus the Numidian funerary traditions of the second century B.C., the double internment, the stairs with their monumental doors, the undersized chambers, and the existence and orientation of the altar, all argue against the identification of Kbor Klib as a mausoleum. And even if the mortuary identification were accepted, we still would not know how to explain the location.

---

[1] Camps notes that the Numidian royal tomb of Khroub was a cremation sepulcher, and speculates that perhaps the Medracen was, as well (Camps 1979: 52), although Ribichini considers burial more likely during the second century B.C. (Ribichini 2001: 142).

A Strictly Religious Sanctuary

Rakob believed that the Chemtou monument functioned principally as a sanctuary to Punic/Numidian, and later to Roman, gods (Rakob 1994: 35). Few investigators have similarly proposed that Kbor Klib was only a high altar or sanctuary. Picard is one, giving this interpretation of Kbor Klib in his last mention of the structure, where he described it as intended to exalt divine glory (Picard 1980: 17). However, he went no further in elaborating this interpretation.

Garcia-Bellido also proposed a purely religious significance for Kbor Klib, as well as for the Chemtou monument, suggesting that both were constructed to honor the goddess Caelestis. She based her hypothesis on supposed associations between that goddess and decorative images on the friezes of arms at both monuments. In the case of Chemtou, the identification with Caelestis is doubtful. Garcia-Bellido argued that a figure on a shield on the recreated façade of the monument (fig. 25), which she said had been identified as "Diana with bow", could be a figure of the goddess Caelestis (Garcia-Bellido 1998: 5-6). However, the artifact was not discovered at Chemtou. It is the shield-born female figure from Kbor Klib, transposed to Chemtou. A shield fragment bearing a carving of a quiver cap, similar to the one on the shield from Kbor Klib, was discovered at Chemtou. However, the recreation of the entire piece, shown on the Chemtou façade recreation, is speculative (Rakob 2005).

In addition, Rakob reported that there was a temple to Caelestis on the summit of the djebel at Chemtou, in addition to the frieze-of-arms monument (Rakob 1994: 40-41, 46). For the Chemtou monument to have been devoted to Caelestis, therefore, two such structures would have existed on the same hilltop, an unlikely circumstance. Finally, votive steles confirm worship of Tanit-Baal, and later Saturn, at the site of the Chemtou monument (Rakob 1994: 34). There is therefore clearly insufficient justification to change the identification of this monument based on Garcia-Bellido's supposition.

For Kbor Klib, Garcia-Bellido's entire argument was that since the female bust displayed on one of the shields recovered there, the same one she believed pertained to Chemtou, might be Caelestis, the entire monument could have been dedicated to her. As all other investigators have identified this female figure as the goddess Artemis (Ferchiou 1991: 54, *inter alia*), and as she offers no other evidence, the hypothesis is not persuasive.

The location of Kbor Klib is problematic for a religious structure. As Picard noted, most ancient religious sanctuaries were associated with population centers, and the suggestion of a sizeable community anywhere near Kbor Klib is entirely speculative. For Chemtou, although there was a Numidian town situated near the monument, which potentially controlled the crossing of the Bagradas river, and therefore trade going to or from the Algerian hinterland (Rakob 2005), there was no major population center nearby. However, Chemtou dominates a lone hill (fig. 39) set at the edge of an area of the middle and upper Bagradas known as the Great Plains, which includes extensive agricultural terrain. The geographic uniqueness of the hill makes it not unlikely that it was perceived as suitable for religious rites, particularly if these rites were associated with agricultural productivity. Additionally, the yellow marble constituting the bedrock underlying the entire hill (the *giallo antico* of the Romans) has been quarried since antiquity, and may have added some degree of sanctity to the setting. The religious significance of the location is confirmed by the existence, during the Roman period, of three temples on the hill (Rakob 1994: Abb. 50). The ridge that bears Kbor Klib, however, has no such claims to geographic or geologic distinctiveness. There are more dramatic locations nearby, ones that dominate the landscape much more effectively, if this was the intent.

The similarities in decoration between Kbor Klib and Chemtou, primarily consisting of the elements of the friezes of arms presumed to have ornamented both structures, might also be considered an argument in favor of the former having been a strictly religious structure, as the latter is considered to have been. However, as observed by Ferchiou, there are crucial differences between the two monuments that argue against any such functional association. Among the more important of these is the difference between the doorways at the two monuments. As noted above, the doorway in the Chemtou monument is considered to have been a false door, inset to form a cultic niche, unlike the functioning entries at Kbor Klib, and surmounted by decoration bearing obviously Egyptian influence (fig. 40). Religious structures with false doors, or niches, some surmounted by architraves decorated with elements drawn from the Egyptian repertoire (fig. 41), have a long history in the Phoenician and Punic worlds (Moscati 1986). Frequently these structures featured statues in the niches, but in no case were the false doorways more than that (Bisi 1971: 1971).

Conversely, Kbor Klib had internal corridors containing stairs, and the only two reasonable explanations for these are that they led either to chambers within the structure, or allowed access to the top of the monument. Nothing similar is proposed for Chemtou, which is considered to have been a solid mass. Certainly there would have been no place for stairs leading to the summit (Rakob 2005). Kbor Klib had a subordinate structure in front of it which is regarded as an altar. Rakob's reconstruction of the Numidian phase of the Chemtou monument does not include an altar (fig. 42). Despite the superficial similarities, therefore, the differences between the two structures are significant enough to argue against the accepted interpretation of Chemtou applying also to Kbor Klib.

There is thus no compelling reason to consider that Kbor Klib was constructed for a purely religious purpose. This is not to suggest that there was no religious significance to the monument. Considering the period of construction, and the structure that is considered to have been an altar, it is inconceivable there was not. However, the martial decorations, the stairs, and the difference from all other known classical temples, indicate that there must have been an additional significance.

Fig. 39. Hilltop location of the monument at Chemtou.

*Fig. 40. Recovered architrave on reconstructed monument in Chemtou museum,
showing Egyptian influence*

Fig. 41. Punic stele, 4th – 3rd century B.C. (Moscati 1997: 435)

In Commemoration of the Clash of Arms

The identification of Kbor Klib as a monument commemorating a military victory, or territorial conquest, has a lengthy history. The recovered shields, cuirasses and weapons immediately convinced the earlier investigators that the monument must have had a martial connotation. They therefore immediately abandoned a funerary attribution for Kbor Klib. A mistaken chronology, combined with the location of the edifice, led some of these investigators to propose a monument constructed in commemoration of the deeds of Caesar. This attribution became untenable once the date of construction was recognized to be some 100 years earlier than the Caesarian period, but the idea of some military connection was never abandoned.

Ferchiou speculated that Kbor Klib was a mausoleum. In her reconstruction of the monument, however, she kept the frieze of arms, and did not ignore the martial significance of this decorative device. She observed that in its original use the frieze represented the weapons of the victors, or of the vanquished, in some military engagement (Ferchiou 1991: 84). For Kbor Klib, even she was willing to entertain a connection to a military conquest, in this case a territorial seizure by Massinissa (Ferchiou 1991: 95-96).

Fig. 42. Reconstruction of Numidian phase of Chemtou monument,
with no structure in front. (Rakob 1994: Abb. II)

43

Polito emphasized the martial nature of the decoration of Chemtou and Kbor Klib, regardless of the possibility of a funerary function. He believed that both monuments principally commemorated the Numidian participation in the Macedonian Wars, and in the case of Kbor Klib Polito argued that the Macedonian iconography used in the decoration was sufficient to confirm the connection.

The recognition of Macedonian influence in the decoration of Kbor Klib is not new. In 1948 Picard described the round shields discovered there as "d'emblème national au royaume de Philippe et d'Alexandre", and suggested that therefore the monument commemorated successes including "un au moins remporté sur des troupes macédoniennes" (Picard 1948: 422-423). In 1957 Picard reiterated the association, noting the similarity between the female bust on the shield recovered from Kbor Klib and figures of Artemis on Macedonian coins issued following the defeat of the last Macedonian king (Picard 1957: 213). The similarity between the hair buns, the neck tresses, and the quiver caps on the figures is striking, even considering the different facing directions of the figures, and the missing bow on the Kbor Klib example (*Fig 43*). Polito also noted the similarity between the Kbor Klib Artemis and the Macedonian coinage. However, where Picard, and after him Ferchiou, noted influences from other cultures in the arms recovered from the monument, Polito saw exclusively Macedonian inspiration. The shield of the Artemis figure, for instance, rests on diagonal carven swords with bird-head decorated grips (*Fig. 43b*, upper right; *Fig. 22*, above). Picard called this sword "l'arme de la cavalrie orientale, iranienne en particulier" (Picard 1957: 213), while Ferchiou observed that the bird head decoration would be "d'origine illyrienne" (Ferchiou 1991: 83-84). Polito only noted that this type of sword was diffused during the Hellenistic era as an arm of prestige (Polito 1999: 44).

A similar treatment applies to the cuirasses from Kbor Klib. Ferchiou noted the discovery of two different varieties of these, one of an Ionian type, and one of a Pergamon type (Ferchiou 1991: 77-79). Again, Polito referred to them only as Hellenistic (Polito 1999: 44).

*Figs. 43a & 43b. Macedonian coin, 158–150 B.C.,
bearing the head of Artemis, and Artemis bust from Kbor Klib.
(coin image taken from http://www.athina.ch/GR/GR07/big88.htm,
Artemis bust Picard 1957: Pl. VI)*

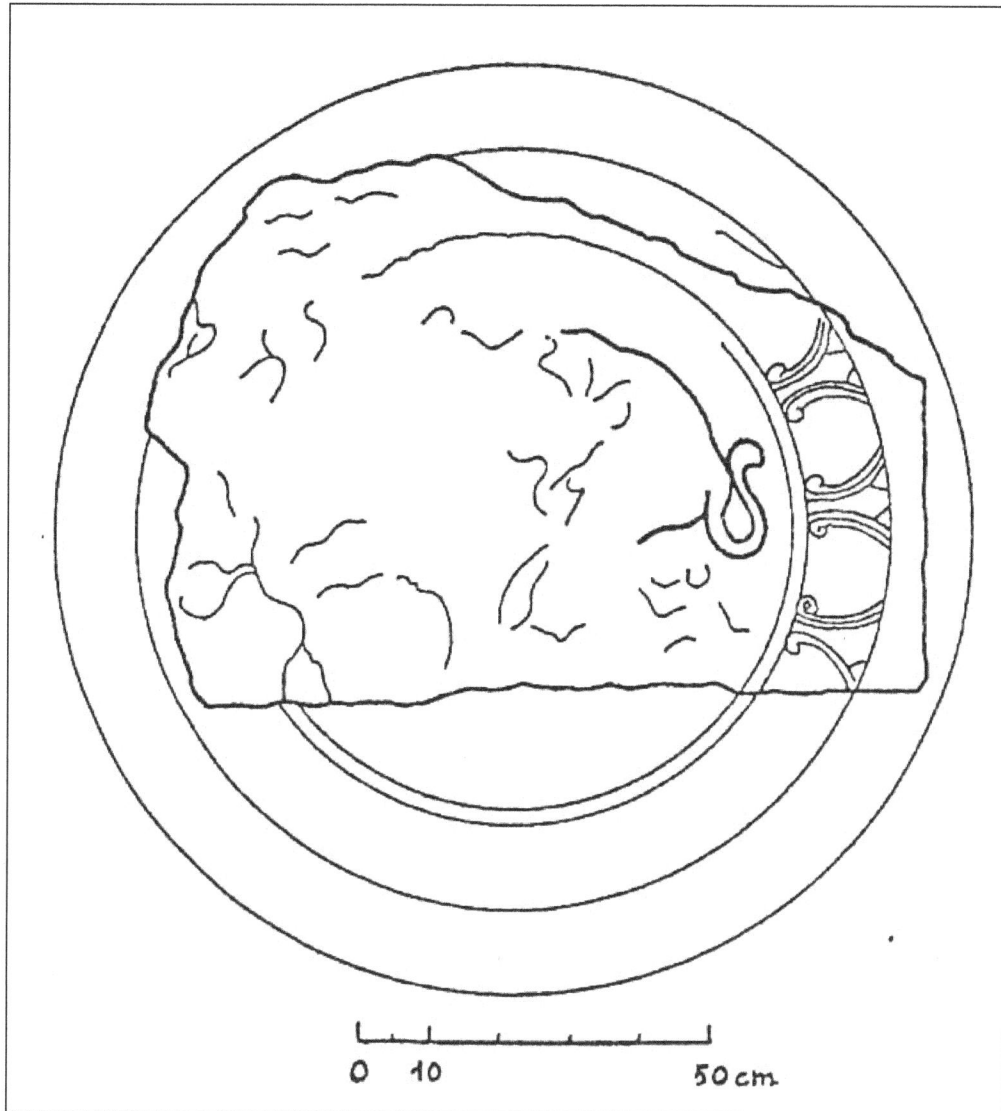

Fig. 44. Shield fragment bearing hindquarters of feline figure. (Ferchiou 1991: Fig. 47)

The pattern continues with a second decorated shield recovered at Kbor Klib, which bears the hindquarters of a feline figure. Ferchiou speculated the figure was a lion, perhaps leaping onto the back of another animal (*Figs. 44 & 22*, above). She reported that this motif "apparaît dès l'époque hellénistique et continué à travers toute l'époque romaine" (Ferchiou 1994: 81-82). Polito, however, argued that the lion figure, which he considered might be solitary, should be given a specifically Macedonian rather than a generalized Hellenistic attribution (Polito 1999: 58-59).

In Polito's hypothesis, this Macedonian iconography could only commemorate Numidian involvement on the side of Rome in the Macedonian Wars. Although the identification of a Macedonian influence seems fairly secure, as noted by earlier investigators, it does not appear so pervasive as to explain Kbor Klib, nor do all other interpretations of this influence seem excluded. Picard, for example, after noting influences in the frieze of arms other than Macedonian, speculated, "l'artiste a voulu donner l'impression d'un amas confus d'armes"

(Picard 1957: 214). Perhaps other interpretations could explain a Macedonian influence in elements of the frieze of arms. Ultimately a crucial question regarding an attribution of Kbor Klib as a monument to the Numidian participation in the Macedonian Wars is why it was built here, in this isolated location in the Tunisian countryside.

A Monument to Numidian Royalty

This paper has proposed that the evidence suggests that the Numidian royal family pursued a building program in order to confirm its power and legitimacy. Ferchiou noted that both the monument at Chemtou and at Kbor Klib were the result of the same coherent political program (Ferchiou 1991: 75). It could therefore be argued that Kbor Klib was simply the product of the efforts of the rulers of Numidia to place their stamp of lordship on the Numidian countryside, one of possibly a number of such structures distributed throughout the kingdom.

Some time before 1926 an inscription in the Punic/Libyan language was discovered at Dougga, Tunisia, which reported the construction there of a temple, during the reign of the Numidian king Micipsa (Frank 1926: 58). This temple had been constructed to honor the memory of Micipsa's father, Massinissa (Brett & Fentress 1997: 38-39). The monument at Chemtou is also conjectured to have been built during the reign of Micipsa. It is thus possible that these two structures represent remnants of the Numidian royal building program, with Kbor Klib being yet another.

Dougga was a significant community during the Numidian era, and it is unsurprising for evidence to have surfaced confirming that a monument honoring the royal family had been constructed there. The inscription dedicating the temple bore the names of the members of the local community responsible for its construction, confirming the interest of these elements of society in associating themselves with the ruling house.

Any association between the Chemtou monument and Micipsa must be based solely on the proposed chronology, which places the construction of the monument during his reign. No dedication from this ruler, or to his father, remains, nor any evidence to confirm that the Chemtou monument was built by the local elites to demonstrate their allegiance to and affiliation with the national leadership, as the temple at Dougga had been.

None of this is to argue, however, that there was no connection between the Numidian royal family and the monument at Chemtou. Chemtou is a significant structure, located on Numidian territory, and even if it had been built at the cost and under the direction of members of the local community, there would presumably have been at least an approval from the king, or his local governor. A more likely scenario is that it was indeed constructed with some involvement of the ruler, if not at his direct behest. Chemtou is considered to have been a religious monument, and involvement in its construction would demonstrate the benevolence, sanctity and power of the royal family.

The same sort of logic applies equally to Kbor Klib. Certainly there would have been some sort of royal approval of the monument, even in the implausible event that it was not the actual work of the king, or other member of the royal family or nobility. Equally certainly, the construction would have represented some sort of political statement, whatever its other functions. The question, though, is whether a royal building program is sufficient in itself to explain the size, unique construction, martial decoration, and location of Kbor Klib. It seems to stretch credulity to propose that Kbor Klib was built where it was, at this distance from the Numidian centers of power, simply to enhance and celebrate the grandeur of the Numidian royal family. This is not to argue that it would not have served these purposes, only that another factor would seem required to explain the location. In other words, why was it considered important to build Kbor Klib here?

Summary

We are thus looking at a monument that might be a mausoleum, but resembles none of the known ones. We have a structure with obvious religious significance, but not a temple or shrine *per se*, nor seemingly attributable to any particular deity. We have decorations that are clearly martial in nature, but the only war we can ascribe them to took place at the other end of the Mediterranean. We have a building that would certainly celebrate the might of the Numidian royal family, but would serve that purpose much more effectively elsewhere. And when our investigators ask themselves why Kbor Klib was built here, isolated in the Tunisian countryside, Saumagne, Déroche, Picard, Ferchiou and Polito all suggest "Zama".

Chapter 4
Looking for Zama

Zama, the City

The Numidian city of Zama enters the existing written record with Polybius, who reported that Hannibal camped there before the battle that ended the Second Punic War. Zama is mentioned in this connection by Livy, Cassius Dio, Appian, and by Cornelius Nepos, who 150 years after the event was responsible for the battle being given that name (Encyclopedia Britannica: Zama). The city is referred to by Sallust (57) in connection with the 111 – 105 B.C. war between Rome and the Numidian king Jugurtha, when it is clearly a Numidian royal city. Cassius Dio (xlviii. 23) and Strabo (xvii. 309) reported that Zama was taken by the Romans and destroyed in 41 B.C., during the Civil War (Walbank 1967: 448). However, the city was evidently rebuilt, as Vitruvius and Pliny mentioned it later (Ennabli: 1), and a Zama Regia is shown on the Peutinger Table (fig. 45), which contains information dating from no earlier than the first century A.D. (Siebold 1998).

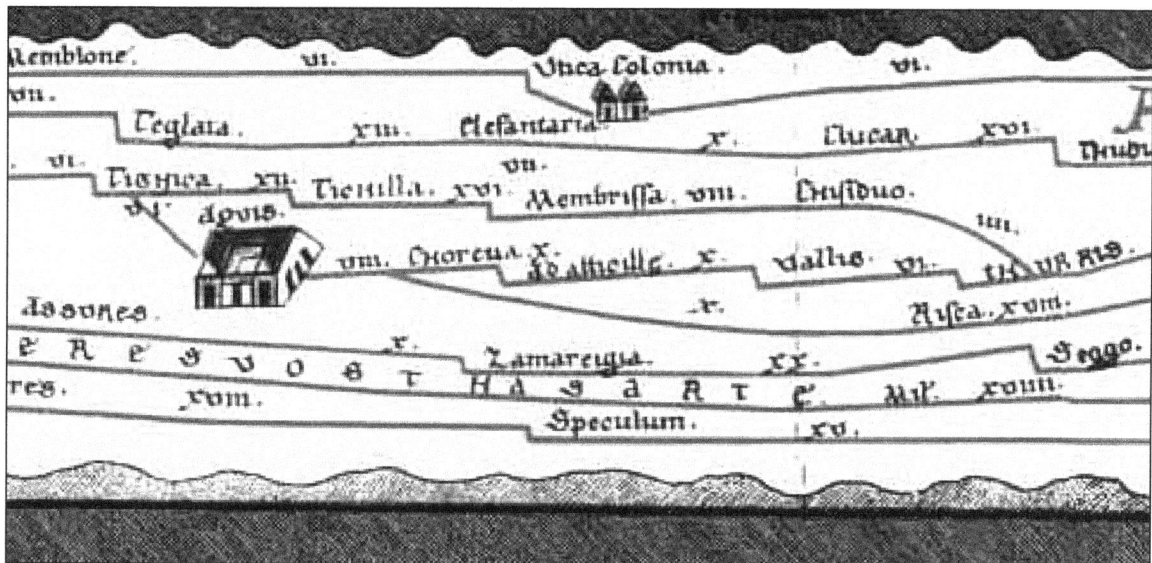

Fig. 45. Peutinger Table, showing section Assuras - Zamaregia - Seggo, third route from bottom, with distances between these towns of X and XX.

The information offered by the ancient writers regarding the location of Zama is slight. Polybius placed it five days journey west of Carthage (15.5.3). Sallust stated, "This town, built on a plain, was better fortified by art than by nature" (57). Pliny (31.12) and Vitruvius (8.3.24) noted its waters were believed to beautify the voice. Vitruvius reported that it was enclosed by double defensive walls built by the Numidian king Juba (Vitruvius: 8.3.24). The Peutinger Table placed it at ten Roman miles from the ancient town of Assuras, and twenty from Seggo.

Because of its connection with the famous battle, the city has attracted considerable attention by modern scholars. Using the information from the ancient accounts, these scholars have attempted to locate the ancient Zama. Francis Russell reports that as early as 1813 the then U.S. consul to Tunisia spent time searching for the location of Zama (Russell 1970: 121). Already in 1854 the Dictionary of Greek and Roman Geography was able to give a concise explanation of the relevance of the ancient city of Zama, noting that it had been known as Zama Regia, or Zama the royal. This article placed Zama Regia at the present day town of Jama, in modern Tunisia (fig. 46), without providing an explanation for the association (Smith: Zama).

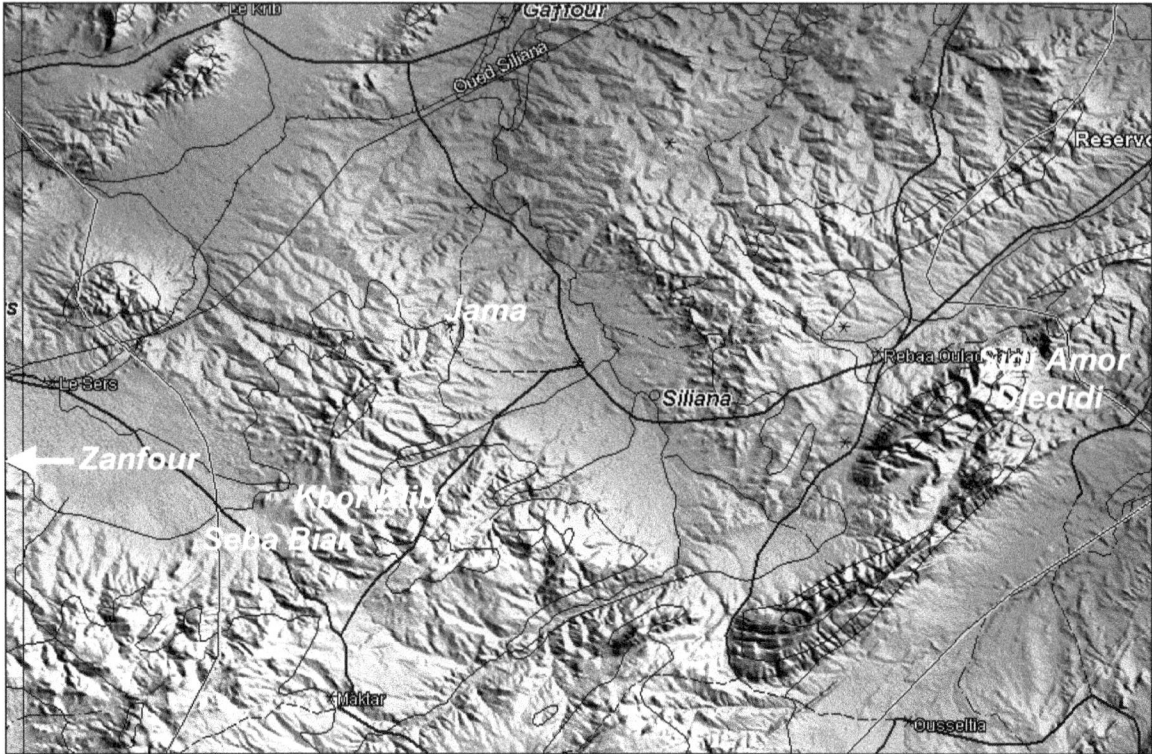

Fig. 46. Kbor Klib, with Seba Biar - 7km SW, Jama 20km - NE,
and Sidi Amor Djedidi - 75km E.

Bostock and Riley, translating Pliny the Elder in 1855, noted that there had been two cities named Zama in the Roman province of Africa. In their opinion, one of these was five days journey west of Carthage, as reported by Polybius, and was the town associated with the famous battle. The other was the town of Zama Regia, residence of the Numidian kings, and located at a site bearing the modern name of Zowarin (Pliny: Ch. 4, footnote 33). Mommsen, in Volume III of his history of Rome, placed Zama not far from the ancient Roman town of Sicca Veneria, the modern El Kef (Mommsen 1856: III, VI, footnote 5).

Brunon, writing in 1887, once again associated the Zama of the battle with Zama Regia, a position adopted nearly universally by subsequent researchers. He favored Jama as the location of this Zama. His arguments in support of the attribution included the description given by Sallust, as Brunon believed Jama would have required walls to protect it, not having been built on an elevated position. Brunon also believed that Jama could be reconciled with the Peutinger table location given for Zama Regia, and that it coincided with the distance from Carthage given by Polybius (Brunon 1887: 7-8).

Cagnat and Saladin, reporting in 1887 on their travels through Tunisia, examined the question of the location of Zama. They observed that popular opinion had generally favored Jama as the location of the ancient community. Then, in 1883, a survey party had discovered in the town of Sidi Amor Djedidi, in central Tunisia (fig. 46), an inscription bearing the name of Zama. The possibility had thus arisen that Sidi Amor was the ancient Zama. Cagnat and Saladin, however, noted that Sidi Amor did not appear to have been significant enough in antiquity to have been a Numidian royal city, and was located too far south to correspond to the distance given from Carthage. Therefore, they reported, opinions remained divided pending further evidence. This evidence took the form of another inscription, discovered at Jama some time between 1883 and 1887, which also bore the name Zama. These inscriptions confirmed that there must indeed have been two Zamas, as earlier proposed by Bostock and Riley. According to these authors, the larger, more important community would have corresponded to Jama, and a smaller Zama would have been at Sidi Amor. Having concluded that the Zama famous for its association with the battle must have been located at Jama, Cagnat and Saladin proceeded to describe their visit to the modern village, noting the significance of the remaining ruins, and, particularly, the quality and quantity of the water still available from the Roman era spring (Cagnat & Saladin 1887: 260).

Toussaint, writing in the *Bulletin archéologique du Comité des Travaux historiques et scientifiques* in 1899, was apparently the first to propose still another location for Zama Regia. He observed that the distances given in the Peutinger table between Zama Regia and Assuras, known to be the modern Zanfour, could not be reconciled with Jama. However, he noted that there was another location, on the Plain of Sers, which could be matched to the Peutinger table location. This was the modern community of Seba Biar (fig. 46), located on the edge of the Plain of Sers and therefore better suited than Jama to the description of Sallust. Toussaint suggested that if Seba Biar was not Zama Regia, it must have been at least the postal station for Zama. Zama itself, he believed, might still have been located at Jama (Ferjaoui 2002: 1005). Based upon the Toussaint hypothesis, the Atlas Archeologique de la Tunisie reflected Seba Biar as possibly the "station postale de Zama Regia (Cagnat & Merlin 1920: Maktar page.)

Pareti, writing in 1911, repeated that there were in antiquity at least two communities in Roman Africa bearing the name of Zama, and possibly three. He described in detail the epigraphic evidence, only mentioned by Cagnat and Saladin, confirming the dual place names. This evidence indicated that in addition to Zama Regia, there had been a community known as Zama major. Consequently, there may also have been a community known as Zama minor. If Zama Regia was not also Zama major, then there would have been three communities known as Zama; Regia, Major and Minor.

The inscriptions confirming the homonyms included the one from Jama, which mentioned *"Zama Ma[..]o[.]"*, as well as the one from Sidi Ahmor Djedidi, which named *"colonia Zamensis"*, a town referenced in an ecclesiastical document of the 4th century (Walbank 1967: 448). Pareti argued that Jama could not have been Zama Regia, as it was in country too hilly to match the description of that city given by Sallust (fig. 47)[1]. He believed that Jama most likely was the ancient Zama major. In his opinion Sidi Ahmor Djedidi also was in terrain unsuitable for the location of Sallust's Zama Regia, and was in any case too insignificant to have been the Numidian royal city. Sidi Ahmor therefore was likely the ancient Zama minor. Both Jama and Sidi Ahmor, Pareti believed, lay within the region controlled by Zama Regia, without either one of them having been the city itself. He therefore believed that three ancient communities bore the name of Zama (Pareti: 304-305).

Having rejected the modern communities of Sidi Amor and Jama as candidates for Zama Regia, Pareti set about determining what other location might better match the descriptions of the ancient sources. He based much of his discussions on the Peutinger Table, and while he could not completely reconcile the distances between the ancient communities given in that document with the distances between their supposed modern counterparts, Pareti felt there was sufficient correlation to confirm his exclusion of Jama as the former Zama Regia. Instead, he proposed that the Peutinger Table supported the identification of Seba Biar as the location of Zama, and, like Toussaint, reinforced this proposal by observing that Seba Biar was located in country

---

[1]   It is interesting to note that where Brunon finds the location of Jama sufficiently flat to match Sallust's description, Pareti finds it too hilly.

Fig. 47. View of modern Jama, looking NW, with ruins of Zama Regia behind.

sufficiently flat to conform to Sallust's description of the city having been located on a plain. In a footnote, Pareti reported that another investigator, Kromayer, had in 1908 identified Seba Biar with Zama Regia, but without, according to Pareti, giving the basis for the association. He did not report Toussaint's earlier association of these two place names. (Pareti 1911: 312-319).

The identification of Seba Biar as Zama Regia acquired authority following articles written by Kromayer himself, allied with fellow investigator Veith, in 1912 and 1922. These articles, particularly the first, also used the Peutinger Table and the Sallust description to support the candidature of Seba Biar. Veith, in an effort to reconcile the two proposed locations for Zama Regia, hypothesized that Zama Regia was originally at Seba Biar. After the city was destroyed during the Roman civil war, the inhabitants relocated to Jama, taking the old name with them. Under this scenario both Seba Biar and Jama were Zama, one the Numidian community and the other the Imperial Roman city (Scullard 1970: 271-272). Déroche, however, flatly rejected this supposition. He reported that Numidian coins were common at Jama, indicating the city existed before the proposed relocation from Seba Biar. Predating the relocation, Jama was unlikely to have been renamed by the evacuees (Déroche 1948: 100-103). Picard additionally noted that modern Jama covered the ruins of important early Numidian monuments (Picard 1967: 205). The existence of these ruins has been confirmed by current excavations at Jama, carried out since 1995 by a Tunisian team of archaeologists headed by A. Ferjaoui. These excavations have recovered Punic coins and ceramics dating back to the 4th century B.C. and a stele dating to the second century B.C (Ferjaoui 2001: 838 & 860-861). This evidence confirms that, if Jama had been Zama Regia, it must have been both the Roman and the Numidian cities of that name. Zama Regia could have been at Jama, or at Seba Biar, but not at both locations.

In 1941 new epigraphic evidence became available that allowed Saumagne, as noted above, to propose present-day Ksar Toual Zouameul as the location of Zama Regia. The inscriptions on which he based his argument, excavated by the proprietor of both Ksar Toual and Kbor Klib, did indeed mention *"Col Zam Reg"* and *"[.]am Reg"*. In addition to the inscriptions, Saumagne argued that the Peutinger Table supported the Ksar Toual attribution, and that the pass between the valleys of Siliana and Sers was suitably level to correspond with Sallust's description of the location of Zama Regia (Saumagne 1941: 250).

However, the identification of Zama Regia with Ksar Toual was short lived, as in 1948 Déroche, reporting on his excavations there, argued convincingly against the attribution. He had recovered numerous additional inscriptions, and thorough study of this material allowed him to conclude that Ksar Toual was the relatively insignificant *Vicus Maracitanus*. The references to Zama Regia contained in the inscriptions studied by Saumagne reflected that *Maracitanus* was in the territory of the royal city of Zama, not that it was that city. Déroche further observed that the ruins at Ksar Toual did not compare to the more significant cities of the region, and were therefore unlikely to be the remains of a Numidian capital. Additionally, there were no signs of the fortifications which Vitruvius had reported surrounding Zama Regia. Ksar Toual could therefore be ruled out as Zama Regia.

Having rejected Ksar Toual as Zama Regia, Déroche spent the second half of his excavation report summarizing the current state of investigation into the location of Zama Regia. Using the Peutinger Table and the descriptions in the ancient sources, like those before him, combined with arguments associated with the boundaries of the Roman north African provinces, Déroche, also like previous investigators, concluded that Zama Regia lay either at Jama, or, more likely, at Seba Biar. Thus Seba Biar once again resumed its position as the leading candidate for the much-sought city.

However, the identification of Seba Bair as Zama Regia had always been problematic, as it was not supported by any physical evidence. It had no significant Roman era remains, containing only "les ruines mediocres" (Saumagne 1941: 237), while Zama Regia is known to have been a Roman city of some consequence (Scullard 1970: 272). There were no signs of defensive walls. Nor had any epigraphic evidence been discovered to support the attribution (Déroche 1948: 104). Seba Biar therefore depended for a connection to Zama solely on the interpretation of ancient texts, one of which, the Peutinger Table, was "très suspectes" (Déroche 1948: 93). The alternate location, Jama, at least had substantial ruins, as well as an inscription, to support its identification as Zama Regia, even if it was possible to interpret some of the available documentation as arguing against this attribution.

More recent investigators have been divided between Seba Biar and Jama as the location of the Numidian Zama Regia, or have suspended judgment pending further evidence. Scullard (1970: 271-272) and Lazenby (1998: 218), for example, favor Seba Biar, while Picard (1967: 205) and Lancel (1995: 173-173) prefer Jama, and the Encyclopedia Britannica suspends judgment.

In 2002, further evidence came to light which seems conclusively to resolve the question of the location of Zama Regia. This evidence consists of another Roman-era inscription, discovered during the ongoing excavations at Jama. The fractured inscription clearly bears the words "Zamen[...] Reg[...]" (fig. 48). The archaeologist in charge of the dig, A. Ferjaoui, presented an account of the discovery to the *L'académie des inscriptions & belles-lettres* in October 2002 (Ferjaoui 2002).[2]

Ferjaoui's article argues convincingly that the location of Zama Regia is now confirmed. And indeed, in combination with the earlier inscription, the place name, and the significance of the site, this new evidence is compelling. Ferjaoui explains at length how Jama can be reconciled with the Peutinger Table distances between Zama Regia and other ancient communities. He

---

[2]   As of 14 December 2003 the inscription remained at the storehouse of the dig site in Jama, where the author was allowed to view it.

also describes how the geography surrounding Jama can be reconciled with the Sallust description of the location of ancient Zama, particularly considering the change in size the community would have undergone over the centuries. These explanations easily overcome the objections raised by earlier researchers against the attribution of Jama as Zama. It now seems finally and firmly resolved that Jama, overlooking the Plain of Siliana, was the Roman, and hence the Numidian, Zama Regia.

The resolution of the location of Zama Regia is significant for the investigation of Kbor Klib. Most researchers had suggested a connection between Kbor Klib and the city of Zama Regia, based mainly on the possibility that Zama Regia was at Seba Biar, on the Plain of Sers below the monument. With the confirmation that Zama was at Jama, to the east of Kbor Klib, this explanation for the position disappears. As Ferchiou noted, Kbor Klib "tourne le dos" on Ksar Toual, and consequently on Jama (they both lie to the east of the monument), and was instead connected with "une ville de la plaine du Sers, ou la plaine elle-même" (Ferchiou 1991: 45). Since neither Zama Regia, nor any other significant population center of the Numidian kingdom yet identified, was on the Plain of Sers, we are left searching for the significance of the location, whatever Kbor Klib's function might have been.

Like the other investigators, Ferchiou posited a connection between Kbor Klib and Zama Regia as the explanation for its having been built here. She also suggested an alternate explanation for the location of the monument, the only investigator really to do so. In 153 B.C., late in his reign, Massinissa seized from Carthage a region of central Tunisia known as *Tusca* (Camps 1960: 194), believed to have incorporated the Plain of Sers (Barrington Atlas 2000: Theveste-Hadrumetum Page; Picard 1963: 128-129). Ferchiou speculated that Kbor Klib was constructed to commemorate this territorial acquisition (Ferchiou 1991: 95-96). However, the appropriation of *Tusca* seems to have been a desultory affair, which could have taken 20 years of intermittent action to accomplish, and was only concluded around 153 B.C. (Walsh 1965: 158). Massinissa had earlier in his reign confiscated other Carthaginian territories, including the coastal cities of the *Emporia*, among which was Leptis Magna, "l'une des plus grandes cités phéniciennes d'Afrique" (Camps 1960: 193-194). In 150 B.C. Massinissa destroyed an army of 25,000 Carthaginians (Walsh 1965: 159). By comparison with these events, the gradual assimilation of the Plain of Sers, lacking any significant cities (Fentress 1979: Map 5), seems hardly to warrant a construction such as Kbor Klib. Was there really no other momentous martial event in the vicinity that might justify such a monument?

Zama: The Battle

The principal reason investigators have attempted to determine the location of the city of Zama is its connection with the battle of that name. Yet the ancient accounts considered the most reliable, those of Polybius and Livy, are unambiguous that the battle did not actually take place at Zama.

The initial circumstances are easily summarized. The Roman general Scipio invaded Africa in 204 B.C. and allied with Massinissa. Winning several engagements against the Carthaginians, he began ravaging the countryside under their control. Carthage recalled Hannibal from Italy to oppose Scipio. Marshalling his forces at Hadrumetum (modern Sousse), Hannibal marched to Zama as a preliminary to an engagement with Scipio, or at least in a threatening move against the Roman. At this point complications arise, for Scipio was not at Zama.

*Fig. 48. Zamen[...] Reg[...] Roman-era inscription discovered at Jama,
Autumn 2002. (Ayachi 2003)*

Instead, Polybius reports that Scipio was sacking Carthaginian towns, although without saying exactly where he was carrying out these depredations (Polybius 15.4, 1-2). Modern scholars have almost unanimously concluded that Scipio was preying on towns in the valley of the Medjerda (Bagradas) River (Mommsen 1854: Chapter VI; Encyclopaedia Britannica 2002: Zama, *inter alia*), as this was the Carthaginian heartland, where the impact would be the most severe (fig. 49). Concurrently Massinissa, with the assistance of some of the Roman forces, was engaged in recovering "his paternal kingdom" and adding "that of Syphax to it" (Polybius: 15.4.4), and was thus presumably to the west of Scipio and Hannibal, in the kingdom of the Masaesyli.

Once at Zama, Hannibal sent out spies to find Scipio. According to the ancient sources these spies were captured by the Romans, but instead of being executed were sent back to Hannibal after being given a tour of the Roman camp. In the Polybius account Massinissa rejoins Scipio immediately afterwards (Polybius 15.5.12).

The release of his spies, doubtless along with other considerations, prompted Hannibal to request a meeting with Scipio. Agreeing to the request, Scipio moved his camp from wherever it was (again, presumably in the Medjerda valley, or a tributary) to a town which is named in the ancient accounts, and which logically would have been in the direction of Hannibal. Unfortunately, the ancient accounts disagree on the name of this community, Polybius calling the town Margaron (Walbank 1965: 447), and Livy calling it Naragarra (Livy 30.29). Hannibal then broke his camp at Zama and moved to a site five kilometers from Scipio. The brevity of the ancient descriptions of the relocations of both Scipio and Hannibal clearly suggest that these movements involved short marches (Polybius 15.5.14 & 15.6.2, Livy 30.29), and that Hannibal's new camp was therefore not more than a day or two march from his camp at Zama. The ancient sources tell us that Hannibal and Scipio did meet, but that, to quote Picard, "L'entrevue n'aboutit à rien" (Picard 1967: 206). The next day the armies met, and the Romans came away with the world.

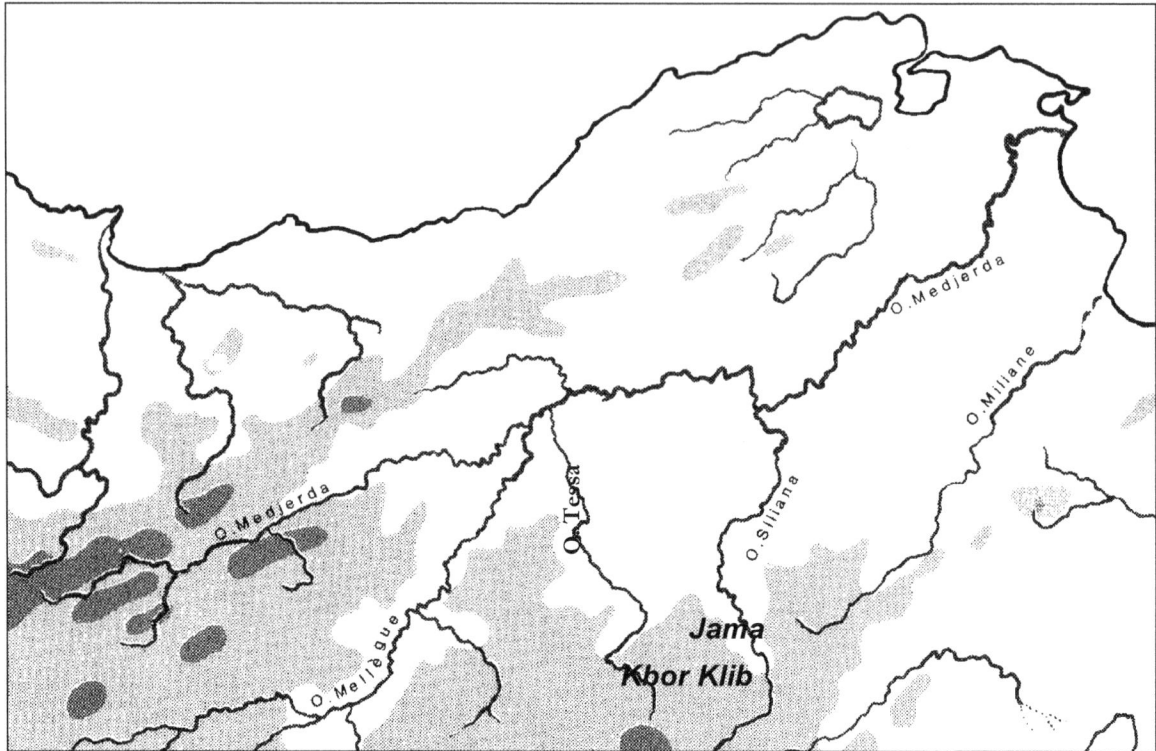

Fig. 49. Map of northern Tunisia showing valley of the Medjerda (Bagradas) River, and routes into central Tunisia, including Oued Miliane, Oued Siliana, Oued Tessa and the Oued Mellègue.

Thus it is not Zama, but Scipio's camp the day before the battle, that locates the ancient battlefield. Modern scholars have been unable to reach a consensus as to the location of this camp. However, two main schools of thought have developed, with one more favored than the other. At issue is the name of the village near which Scipio camped.

The ancient Margaron named by Polybius is not known, but an ancient Naragarra, possibly conforming to the town named by Livy[3], is. This is the modern community of Sakiet Sidi Youssef, west of Le Kef on the border with Algeria (fig. 50). The problem with Sidi Youssef as a battlefield is that the surrounding terrain, for some distance, is too hilly for the engagement described in the ancient sources (Scullard 1970: 272, *inter alia*). In order to overcome the difficulty with the terrain one of the earlier investigators, Pareti, in 1911 proposed that Scipio first camped at Naragarra, then later marched to a location 30 kilometers away, near the modern village of Sidi Zine, and camped close to level terrain there (1911: 310-316). Hannibal moved from Zama to a location nearby, and this was the battlefield. Pareti even picked two hills as the locations of the opposing armies. This hypothesis was built upon by Kromayer & Veith (1922: Blatt 8), who even produced a map of the battle based on Pareti's theory (fig. 51). The theory is either accepted or seriously entertained by Cottrell (1960: 204-209), Walbank (1967: 447), Warmington (1969: 216), Scullard (1970: 273) and Lazenby (1998: 218).

The logic that initially led to the selection of this site is, however, debatable. Livy says Scipio camped at Naragarra, while Polybius says Margaron. Both say the battle was fought there, at the location of this camp. Researchers believe they know where Naragarra was, but do not believe the action could have been fought there. Therefore, they first have Scipio camp at

---

[3]   In fact the surviving texts of Livy do not agree concerning the spelling of the name of Naragarra, with several variations given in the surviving texts (Russell 1970: 122).

Naragarra, and then march another 30 kilometers and camp at another location, where the terrain suits the battle. This additional movement, nowhere reported in the ancient sources, is defended with the argument that the putative second campsite is in the general area of Naragarra, speculation that there might have been another community named Naragarra in the vicinity of Le Kef, and further speculation that there was possibly a community named Margaron nearby (Scullard 1970: 272-273). No line of reasoning is presented to explain why this relocation of the Roman army is unreported in the ancient accounts, and no epigraphic evidence is offered to support either a second Naragarra, or an ancient Margaron, in the area. The location is simply considered suitable due to the terrain.

In addition to the basic contradiction of the Sidi Zine hypothesis with the available documentation, involving as it does a troop movement unrecorded in the ancient accounts, there is now a further objection. When the Sidi Zine site was first proposed, Seba Biar was considered the more likely candidate for Zama, and thus for the site of Hannibal's camp. The Kromayer and Veith map of the routes of Hannibal and Scipio to the battlefield, produced in 1922, clearly indicates Zama at Seba Biar (fig. 52). Jakob Seibert, producing a similar map in 2004, continued to place the Carthaginian forces at Seba Biar before the final advance to meet Scipio (fig. 53). From Seba Biar, this advance would have been marginally short enough to be reconciled with the brief march indicated in the ancient accounts. With the identification of Jama as Zama Regia, however, and the addition of approximately 20 kilometers to the marching distance, such is no longer the case, and the Sidi Zine candidate for the battle of Zama becomes even less plausible when compared with the existing descriptions.

The most popular alternative candidate for the location of the battle of Zama has fewer published adherents. In his 1941 article on Zama Regia, Saumagne noted that a Roman era inscription had been discovered at a location approximately 17 kilometers southwest of Zama Regia (for him, Ksar Toual Zouammel), on the Plain of Siliana, bearing the letters C[...]RAG · SARA. This location was Henchir Chaâr (fig. 54). In evaluating the inscription, Saumagne speculated that it stood for Naragsara, and could have been a corruption, or alternate transliteration, of the name of the community identified by Livy as the site of Scipio's camp (Saumagne 1941: 267-269). In his 1967 book on Hannibal, Picard accepted this analysis, and therefore placed the battle of Zama on the Plain of Siliana. As additional support for this location, Picard noted that the easiest routes into central Tunisia, and thus the routes Scipio was most likely to follow, ran through the Plain of Siliana (Picard 1967: 205-206 & 267).

The Henchir Chaâr location is apparently accepted by the archaeologists who excavated the Zama Regia inscription at Jama. The online EurNews article initially reporting the find quotes Professor Piero Bartoloni, co-director of the dig, as stating that the inscription "ci consente di affermare con assoluta certezza che il sito de Jama è il luogo in cui l'esercito dei Romani sconfisse le truppe di Annibale". Professor Bartoloni goes on to note the suitability of the nearby terrain for the battle. When this author inquired of the archaeological students left in charge of the Jama dig site where they thought the battle took place, they pointed southeast toward the location given by Picard (fig. 55). Thus the Henchir Chaâr site seems the local favorite.

However, there are difficulties with this location, commencing with the inscription. In a 1991 article entitled "Inscriptions découvertes entre *Zama Regia* (Henchir Jâma) et *[Ma]rag(ui) Sara* (Henchir Chaâr)", Ahmed M'charek argued convincingly that the inscription stood for either Maragui Sara or Maraguitana Sara. The Barrington Atlas accepts the identification and reflects this place name on its map of the area. M'charek himself speculated that Maragui Sara might be a corruption of Polybius' Margaron, but the resemblance is not compelling (M'charek 1991: 256-257).

57

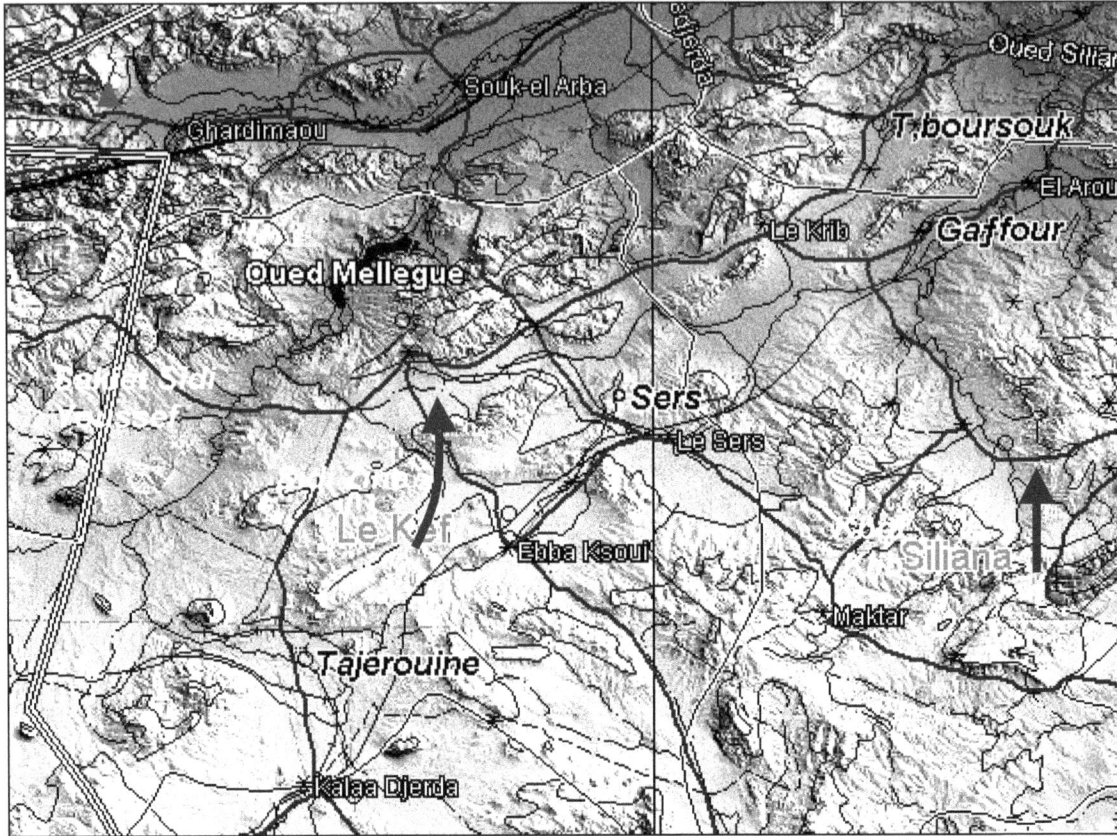

*Fig. 50. Map of NW Tunisia, Sakiet Sidi Youssef – 30km W of Le Kef,
Sidi Zine – 7km SW of Le Kef, Kbor Klib SE.*

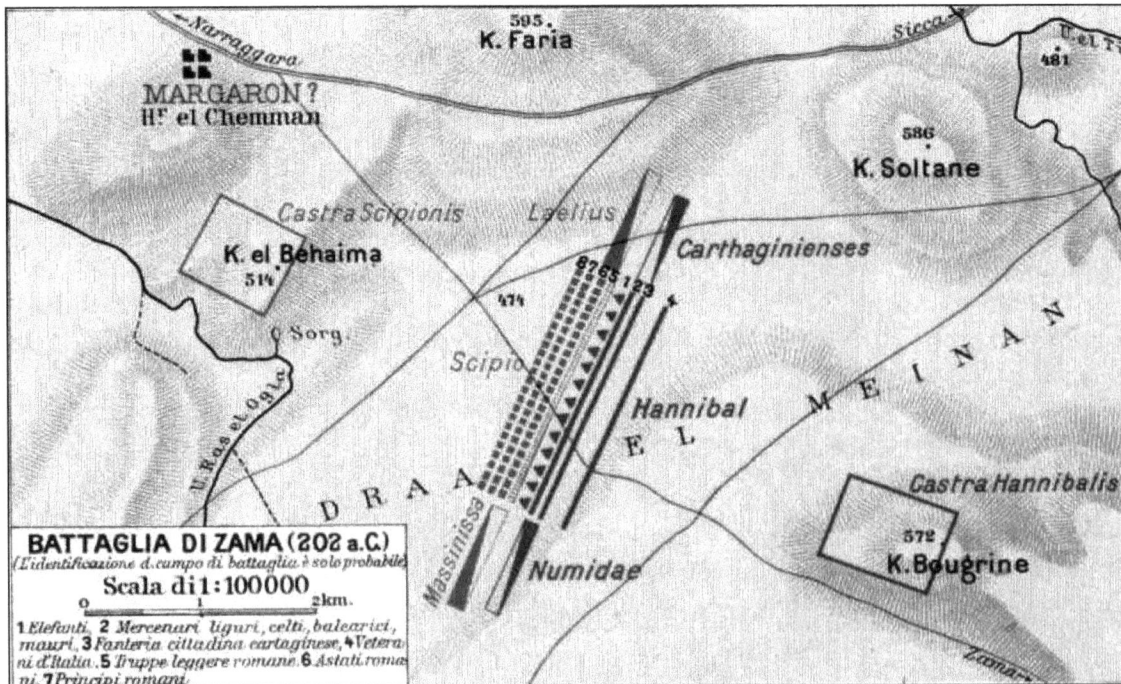

*Fig. 51. Proposed Zama battlefield, following Pareti. (taken from
http://www.barca.fsnet.co.uk/zama.htm)*

58

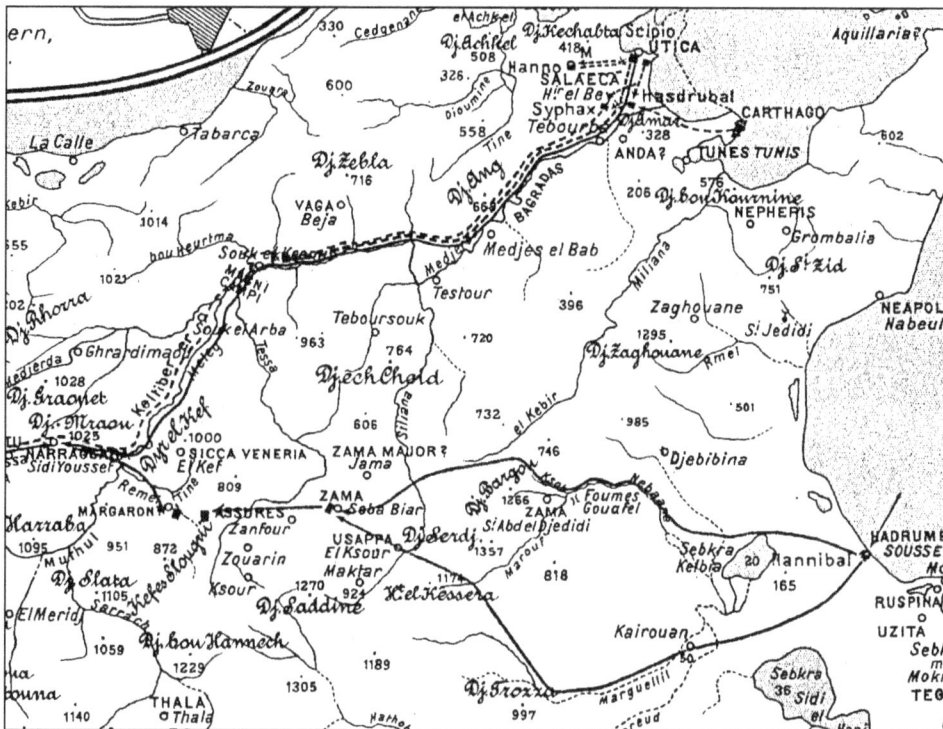

Fig. 52. Routes of Scipio and Massinissa (checked lines) and Hannibal (solid lines)
to proposed Zama battle site near Le Kef, labeled Margaron on the map,
with Zama at Seba Biar. (Kromayer & Veith 1922: Blatt 8)

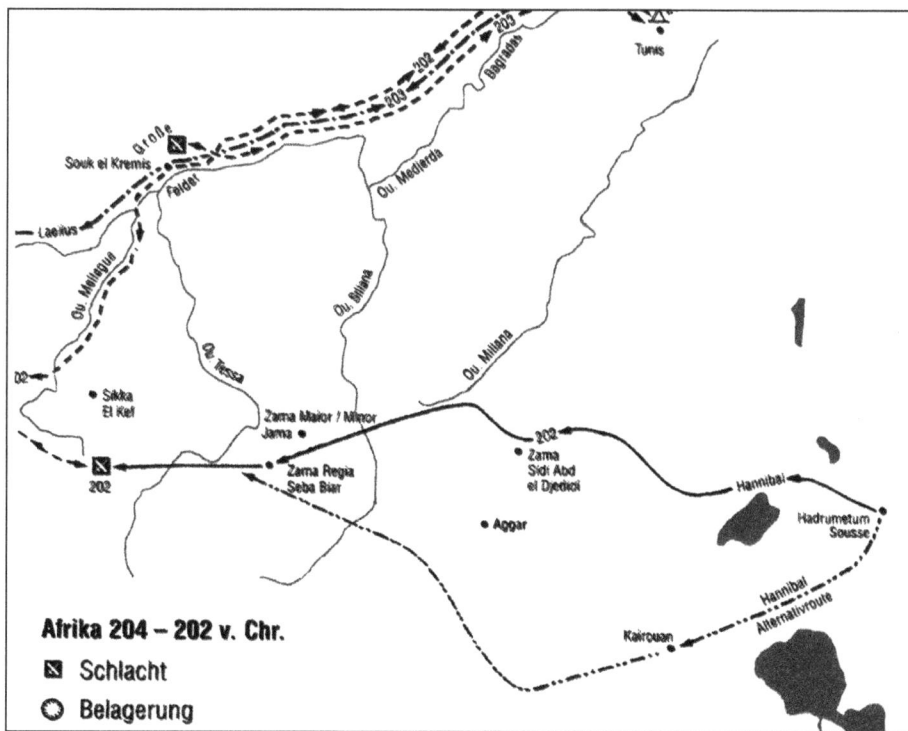

Fig. 53. Routes of Scipio and Massinissa (checked lines) and Hannibal (solid & dotted lines)
to proposed site of battle of Zama, south of Le Kef, with Zama placed at Seba Biar. (Seibert
2004: 32)

More significantly, there are practical reasons to question the location. In his 1970 article on the battle of Zama, Russell observed that Hannibal came west from Hadrumetum to Zama, and his route, a variation on the northern one in figures 51 & 52, above, would have taken him over the range of hills to the southeast of Siliana. From the top of these hills, the entire Plain of Siliana is visible. If they were anywhere on the plain, Hannibal would not have needed to send out spies from Zama to locate Scipio's army of some 25,000 men; he would have seen the Roman forces before he got there (Russell 1970: 127).

Distance is also a difficulty. The Henchir Chaâr site proposed for Scipio's camp is some 15 kilometers from Jama. Hannibal's army would have been camped on the level terrain below Jama, a kilometer or two from the city, so less than 15 kilometers from Henchir Chaâr. It would have been pointless for Hannibal to relocate his camp in order to meet with Scipio; a short horseback ride would have taken him to "a spot...midway between the camps" for the meeting (Livy 30.29). Even to engage in battle, his army could have marched half the distance to Scipio without making an intermediate camp, eight kilometers not being an excessive distance for an army to cover.

With considerable doubt appending to the two most popular candidates for the location of the battle of Zama, now that the location of the city of Zama Regia seems conclusively resolved, we are left wondering if no other site more suitable has been suggested. And there is another candidate.

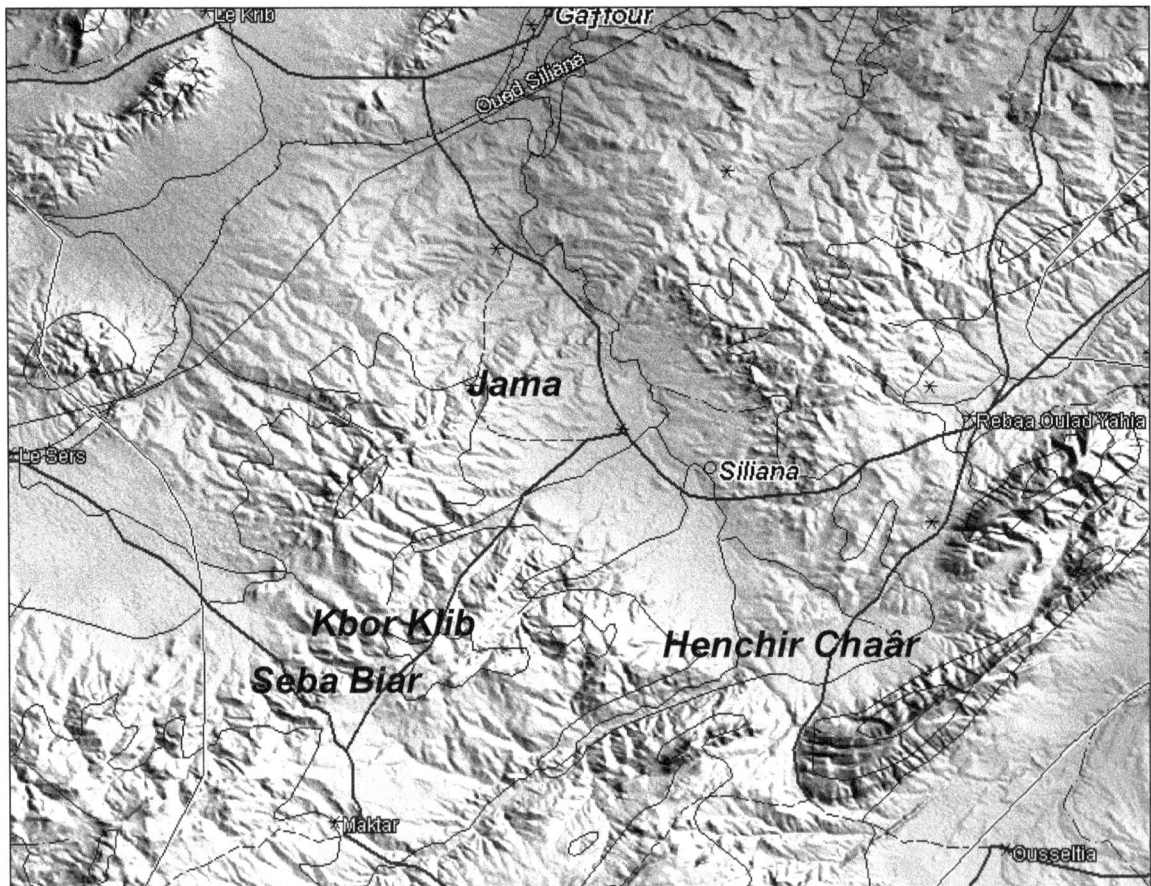

Fig. 54. Putative Henchir Chaâr battle site, south of Siliana, 15km SE of Kbor Klib.

Fig. 55. Plain of Siliana, looking SE from Jama toward proposed Zama battlefield.

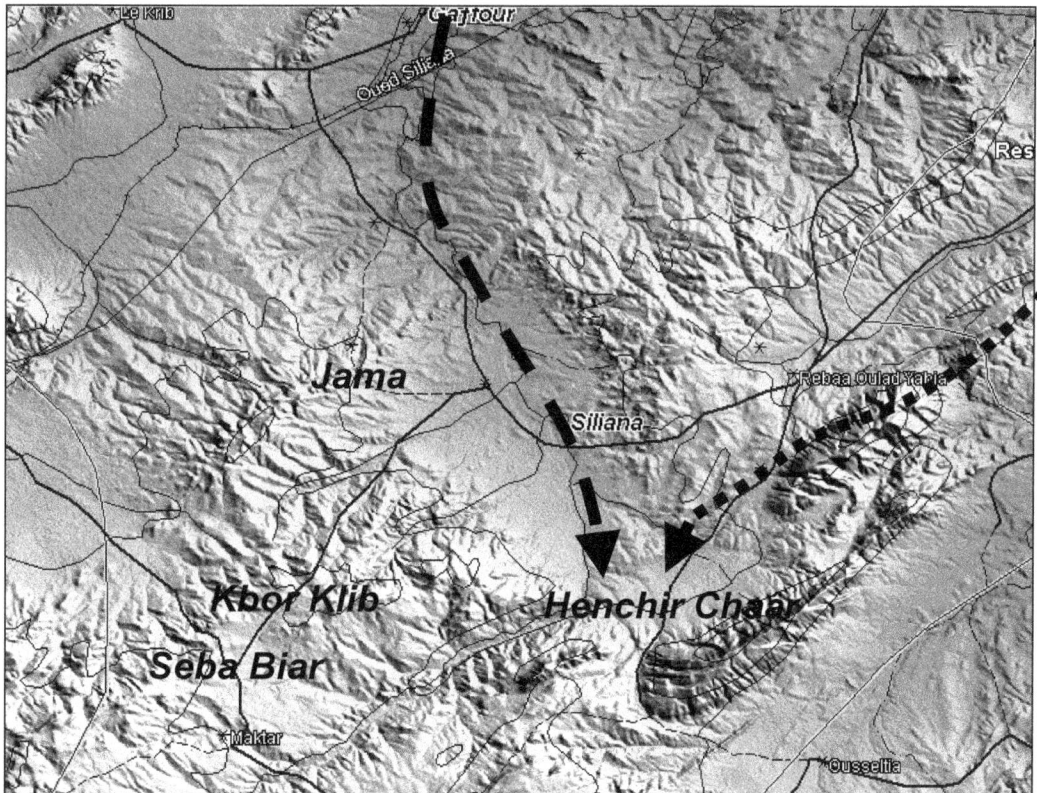

Fig. 56. Scipio's proposed routes to Henchir Chaâr battle site, following Oued Siliana
(checked line) or Oued Miliane (dotted line).
Note proximity to Jama of the Oued Siliana route.

61

In his 1970 article on the battle of Zama, Francis Russell proposed a third site for the battlefield. He suggested that if Scipio was marauding in the Medjerda valley, as most researchers agree, and if he did not turn south into the Oued Siliana (to reach the Plain of Siliana), or continue west past Le Kef (to the Sid Zine site), there was only one other route into central Tunisia he was likely to have used. This is the Oued Tessa, which leads from the Medjerda into the Plain of Sers (figs. 49, above). Thus it is here, near the village of Seba Biar, that Russell, apparently alone among the researchers, places the famous battle (fig. 57).

A Plain of Sers location fits the ancient accounts in critical respects. Modern investigators have questioned why Hannibal would initially have moved to Zama, particularly if Scipio was known to be marauding in the Bagradas valley, much further to the west and north. A quick look at the map (fig. 49, above) reveals the logic of Hannibal's move if, when he decided to take the field against the Romans, he knew that they had left the Bagradas and were moving south up the Oued Tessa. Zama would be the perfect location from which to intercept the enemy. For their part, by moving south up the Tessa the Romans would have been making it more difficult for Hannibal to interpose himself between them and Massinissa, still somewhere to the west. Indeed, this is one of the reasons Hannibal is speculated to have moved west when he did; in order to prevent the Romans from joining with their Numidian allies (Walsh 1970: 141).

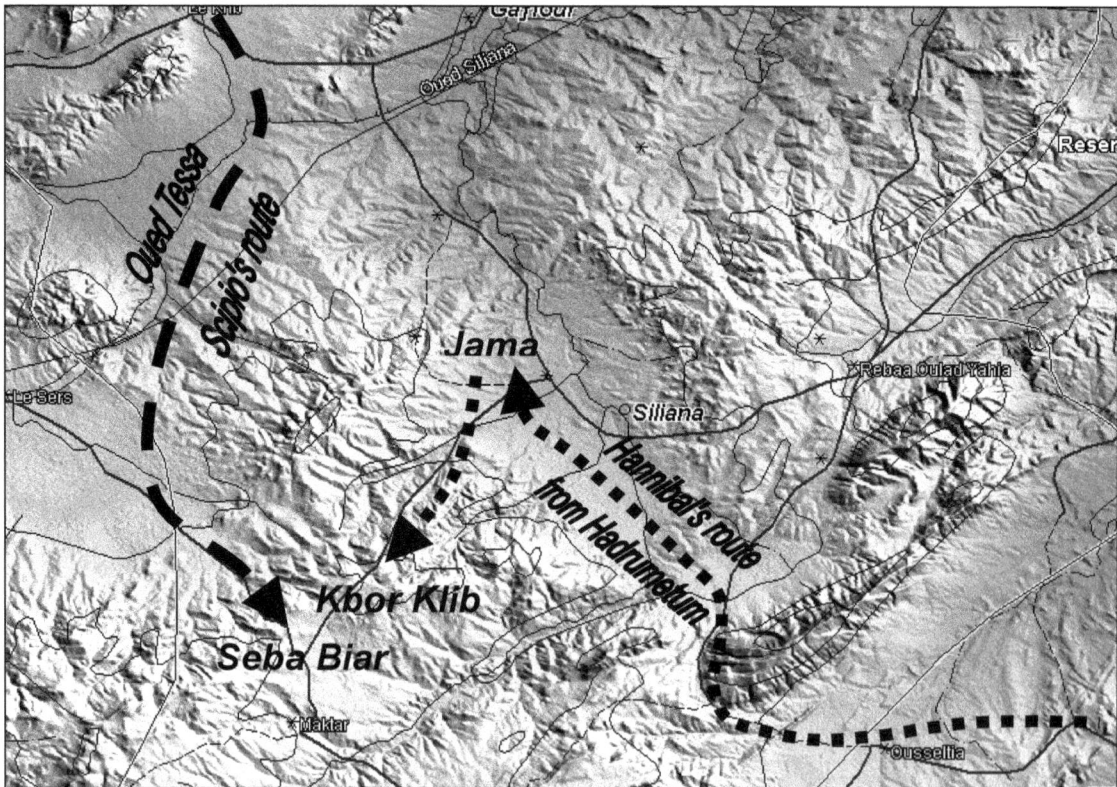

Fig. 57. Hannibal's proposed route to Zama, and then to Kbor Klib,
and Scipio's proposed route to Seba Biar.
Distance between Jama and Kbor Klib is approximately 20km.

However, crossing the Plain of Siliana to reach Zama Regia, Hannibal would not have detected Scipio's army, approaching or on the Plain of Sers, due to the intervening arms of the Djebel Massouges. Once encamped at Zama Regia, sending out spies would have been the logical way to pinpoint his adversary. Following the capture and release of Hannibal's spies, and Hannibal's request for a meeting, Scipio would have continued his southward movement, reaching Seba Biar. Seba Biar is approximately 20 kilometers from Jama; well within the marching distance Walbank reckons a reasonable daily average (Walbank 1967: 449). After Scipio agreed to the meeting, therefore, Hannibal's army would have had a one-day march to the new location. Hannibal could have met with Scipio while his camp was being set up, or on the next day. The day following the fruitless interview the battle would have ensued.

This paper thus proposes that the battle of Zama took place at the southern end of the Plain of Sers, near the village of Seba Biar, a location apparently advanced only by Russell.[4] This paper also proposes that Kbor Klib, a second century B.C. Numidian monument seven kilometers from Seba Biar, bearing martial decorations, and with no good explanation for its being there, was constructed to commemorate the battle of Zama. This connection is not believed to have been previously published[5].

Kbor Klib dominates the slopes of a ridgeline to the east of Seba Biar. As noted by Ferchiou, the monument is hidden when approached from the east. From Seba Biar itself the structure is barely visible on the skyline, and would have been so even at its original height and coloration. Traveling west from Seba Biar on the natural route dictated by the topography, Kbor Klib comes into full view at a point approximately midway between the village and the monument (fig. 58). It seems clearly from here, along a three or four kilometer stretch of country lane, that the monument has significance. And it is specifically here, in the farmland along this same stretch of roadway, that the battle of Zama is proposed to have been fought.

This site suits the limited information given in the ancient sources. Polybius notes that Hannibal, when he moved from Zama to a location near Scipio, camped at 30 stades, or approximately five kilometers, from his adversary (Lazenby 1998: 218). It is proposed that Hannibal camped on the ridgeline where today stand the ruins of Kbor Klib. Scipio is proposed to have camped on the hill shown in the photograph below, taken from the summit of Kbor Klib, looking west (fig. 59). The distance between these two putative camps, measured by GPS, is 4.6 kilometers. It is proposed that the battle was fought here, on the plain between these two locations. This plain rises gently at one end, sloping away at the other, and includes relatively level terrain roughly five kilometers in width, more than wide enough for the four-kilometer long battle lines shown on the Kromayer and Veith reconstruction of the battle (fig. 51, above).

Polybius also noted that the Roman camp was within easy access of water, while the Carthaginians were camped some distance from a source of water, and suffered from thirst as a consequence (15.5-6). The ridgeline where Kbor Klib is located, and where it is argued Hannibal camped, is without surface water during the dry season[6]. Seba Biar, however, where Scipio is argued to have camped, is well watered, the name Seba Biar translating as "seven springs" (Déroche 1948: 98).

---

[4] Cagnat and Saladin, passing through the area in 1887, noted the suitability of the Plain of Sers for the battle site and suggested that perhaps it had taken place there, without exploring the possibility further (Cagnat & Saladin 1887: 254).

[5] This assertion must include a caveat. In his 1967 book on Hannibal, Picard noted "Aussi pensons-nous, malgré l'avis contraire de l'architecte A. Lézine, que le Kbor Klib commémore non la bataille de Zama, mais la prise de cette même ville en l'an 46 av. J.-C. par Cesar." (Picard 1967: 205). It therefore appears that Lézine believed that Kbor Klib commemorated the battle of Zama. However, exhaustive research, not only of Lézine's work on Kbor Klib, but also of other sources where it is possible he formally made some remark to this effect, have proven fruitless. Nor do Ferchiou or Polito, both of whom extensively researched Kbor Klib, and both of whom reference Lézine, report any such theory by him. It appears that Lézine either expressed the opinion privately to Picard, or made it publicly in an unrecorded venue. In any event, while this author independently conceived a connection between Kbor Klib and Zama, he cannot profess to have been the first to do so.

[6] The battle of Zama is traditionally dated to 19 October 202 B.C., which is frequently just before the onset of the wet season, depending on the year.

Thus, in addition to the logic of the advances which would have led the opposing armies to this particular place, the information specific to the battlefield given by the ancient historians also supports these fields as the site of the Battle of Zama. Guarded for 2200 years by the ruined, solitary stone structure of Kbor Klib, this is the landscape, it is proposed, where the Romans sealed their mastery of the Mediterranean world.

Fig. 58. Kbor Klib, taken from what is proposed to be the battlefield of Zama, approximately three kilometers due west, in the direction of Seba Biar.

Fig. 59. Plain of Sers, looking due west from Kbor Klib over proposed Zama battlefield, Scipio's putative campsite on smaller hill in the distance, center.

Chapter 5
Conclusion

Even if the association of Kbor Klib with the battle of Zama were accepted, questions would remain, one of these being the issue of function. There is consensus among researchers that the monument commemorated some martial event or process. However, particularly in consideration of the stairs, the question arises whether it had an additional meaning. For this author, the doubts appending to the identification of Kbor Klib as a mausoleum are severe enough to reject the identification. Instead, Kbor Klib is believed to be primarily a triumphal monument, as proposed by Déroche and Picard (although commemorating a different event). The purpose of the stairs as they relate to this function is unknown. It is possible that they did lead to chambers within the structure, but ones serving purposes other than mortuary. Alternately, as originally assumed by Picard and Lézine, perhaps they did reach the top of the monument, in a configuration not currently evident.

Another question would be the use of the Macedonian influenced elements on the frieze of arms. Here the answer is perhaps straightforward. According to Livy, Hannibal's second line at the battle of Zama included "a legion of Macedonians" (Livy 30.33.5), and although Walbank believes this to be a later invention, he does so based simply on Polybius' failure to mention their presence (Walbank 1967: 456). Hannibal's first line, according to Polybius, consisted of Carthaginian citizens pressed into service. These were unlikely to have been armored with any consistency. In addition to Livy's Macedonians, the second line was composed of mercenaries, and these also were unlikely to have been uniformly armored. In the third and final line of Hannibal's army were his Italian veterans. These would have been using an assortment of weapons mostly captured from defeated Romans (Warry 1980: 122). It would have been impolitic for the Numidians to choose the equipment of their allies to commemorate a joint victory. It would, however, be unsurprising for Macedonian motifs to be represented in the stylized armor decorating a monument to the battle of Zama, whether or not this ally of Carthage contributed an entire legion to her defense, and for the frieze of arms from that monument to resemble Picard's "amas confus d'armes".

As for the question of the name of the community near which Scipio camped, a Seba Biar site for the battle of Zama, and Kbor Klib as a monument commemorating that event, present a plausible solution. Russell argued that the name of Margaron, given by Polybius, was accurate, and that the Naragarra of Livy was perhaps a corruption by a later transcriber familiar with the latter community. As the *Vicus Maracitanus*, or *Vicus Maraci* (M'charek 1991: 259), was only one kilometer from the monument believed to commemorate the battle, it would have been reasonable for Polybius, writing after the monument was constructed, to have used the name of this community to locate the battle. Margaron could therefore be a corruption of *Maracitanus*, or, more likely, of the Numidian precursor to the name of the Roman village.[1]

In fact, one theory holds that neither Polybius nor Livy correctly transcribed the name of the community near which Scipio camped. Davide Nizza, writing in 1980, evaluated both the Greek script of the existing copies of Polybius, and the Latin writing in the extant copies of Livy. He concluded that the names given in these documents were attempts to transcribe from the Punic language a name for which there was no real translation in either of the other languages. He ultimately concluded that a fair approximation of the original name of the town

---

[1] The similarity between Margaron and *Maracitanus* had been noted by Déroche (1948: 82).

near which the battle was fought would be *Nahrgara*. This name, in Nizza's opinion, would have been derived from the Semitic word for water, *nahar*, and would have reflected the proximity to water of Scipio's camp, as reported in the ancient accounts (Nizza 1980: 85-88). The search for a Roman era inscription proving the location of the community named by either Polybius or Livy is therefore potentially futile, although it is worth repeating that the name Seba Biar means seven springs, and perhaps the Punic or Numidian name for that community would have correlated to Nizza's *Nahrgara*.

An issue related to the possible identification of the original function of Kbor Klib concerns its sister monument at Chemtou. As this paper proposes a new explanation for the construction of Kbor Klib, what are the implications for Chemtou? Ferchiou suggested that Kbor Klib was built before Chemtou, a chronology this author accepts. Kbor Klib was thus constructed by and commemorated the deeds of Massinissa. Ferchiou further suggested that Chemtou commemorated the acquisition by the Numidian kingdom of a district known as the Great Plains of the Bagradas Valley, as the monument surmounts a hill which dominates this district (Ferchiou 1991: 95-96). Alternately, the second most important battle of the Second Punic War, after Zama, is known as the battle of the Great Plains, and perhaps the real meaning of Chemtou lies there. Whether Chemtou celebrated a territorial acquisition, or another engagement of the Second Punic War, Kbor Klib, at some three times the size, commemorated the more significant battle of Zama.

The most serious difficulty in associating Kbor Klib with the battle of Zama is chronology. The consensus is that Kbor Klib dates from around the middle of the second century B.C., while the battle of Zama took place in 202 B.C. Why would Massinissa, or his heir if it was built under Micipsa, have waited 50 years to commemorate this seminal event?

One consideration is the secureness of the chronology. Lézine believed Kbor Klib pre-dated the 146 B.C. destruction of Carthage. He did not estimate an earliest possible date for its construction. While Ferchiou supposed a mid-second century B.C. chronology for the monument, neither her ceramic nor stylistic evidence precluded an earlier date. Indeed, she considered that certain stylistic indications suggested a date "assez haute", and from her sondages she recovered one fragment of pottery that "qui serait une production punique des III-IIe s. av. J.C." (Ferchiou 1991: 95). Thus Kbor Klib might very well have been constructed much nearer the time of the battle of Zama than the currently estimated date reflects.

Even if the mid-second century date proved accurate, the delay in the construction of Kbor Klib could reasonably be explained by possession of the terrain. Ferchiou suggested the monument was constructed to commemorate the seizure from Carthage, in 153 B.C., of the territory of *Tusca*, which likely included the Plain of Sers, and thus the proposed Zama battlefield (Ferchiou 1991: 95-96). Alternately, perhaps the territorial acquisition finally allowed Massinissa to build a battle memorial, the site having remained in Carthaginian hands during the intervening years.

Regardless of possession of the terrain, perhaps it was only late in life that an aging king Massinissa decided to memorialize the most momentous event of his reign, indeed one of the most momentous events of Mediterranean history. Alternatively, perhaps his son and successor, Micipsa, wishing to provide a physical reminder of the relevance of the dynasty established by Massinissa, chose to memorialize both the battle and the founder of that dynasty. It is likely that even at the time of the battle of Zama it was recognized as a decisive event. If not, it certainly was 50 years later. Polybius, writing around the time of the Third Punic War, observed that at Zama the Romans were fighting "for the empire of the world" (Polybius 15.9.2). In one interpretation, Massinissa was the real victor over Hannibal at Zama

(Bouchenaki 1979: 85). The Numidian kingdom, wealthy enough to afford an elaborate memorial, wishing to legitimize its position both with the other political elites of the Mediterranean and among its own people, and adopting traditions of the Hellenized states (one of which was monumental architecture), would have been unlikely not to have commemorated her participation in, and critical contribution to, this world capturing event.

The Third Punic War saw the obliteration, by the Romans, of Carthage, still at that time one of the most powerful Mediterranean cultures, and still a dominant force in North Africa. After destroying its rival, Rome expanded its territorial control in the region. The Numidian kingdom supported Rome during the final confrontation with Carthage, and therefore had cause to feel confident in its relationship with its ally. Nonetheless, there must have been some sense of vulnerability, some apprehension, in having the increased presence of an obviously expansionist power right next door. It would not have been surprising for the Numidians to have built a monument commemorating its earlier support for Rome during the far more critical Battle of Zama, as a reminder of its services to the expanding empire.

A problem related to both function and chronology is whether it is plausible to suppose that a Numidian king constructed a monument celebrating a military victory, on the site of the battlefield, in the early second century B.C. Picard, in briefly explaining his rejection of any connection between Kbor Klib and the battle of Zama, wrote in his 1957 book on Roman trophies, "En 202, ni les Romains, ni à plus forte raison les Numides ne bâtissaient de trophées sur le champ de bataille" (Picard 1957: 215). He believed that the tradition of battle monument construction by the Romans, at least, dated from no earlier than 121 B.C. (Picard 1957: 101). Pietilä-Castrén, writing in 1987, evaluated the victory monuments of the Roman generals of the era of the Punic Wars. She described 30 of these structures, nearly all of which were temples, and all of which were built in Rome or its environs. These buildings confirm that Roman generals memorialized foreign military victories, in Rome, undoubtedly for their own political purposes. In the second century B.C., therefore, the identified structures argue against the Romans having commemorated victories with structures located on the battlefield.

In 1990 a Roman battlefield trophy dating from 86 B.C., and celebrating Sulla's victory over Mithridates at the battle of Chaironeia, was discovered in Greece (Camp 1992). In November of 2004 the sister to this monument, also commemorating a Sullan victory, was uncovered by a farmer at Orchomenos (Gatopoulos, D. 2004). These trophies confirm only that the Romans were erecting battlefield victory monuments some 120 years after Zama, and in any case these commemoratives were constructed to resemble the armor of the slain, suspended on a tree trunk (*Fig. 60*). This configuration is very much different from the monument at Kbor Klib. Indeed, when trying to find known battlefield monuments with which to compare Kbor Klib, neither Déroche, Picard, Lézine, Ferchiou nor Polito was able to identify any structure which bore more than the most passing resemblance. The chronology, form and function of known Roman battle trophies seems to confirm that, as asserted by Picard, there was no tradition of battlefield memorials at the presumed time of the construction of Kbor Klib, even for the Roman culture, let alone for the Numidian.

Nonetheless, the fact remains that Kbor Klib was built, and, notwithstanding the superficial similarities to the smaller monument at Chemtou, that it is unique. There is nothing quite like it, anywhere. It must have been built to commemorate, or celebrate, some event, personage, or deity. In any of these roles, it would remain unique. It is therefore not preposterous to suppose that, with a uniqueness in function to match its uniqueness in construction, Kbor Klib is the earliest known battlefield memorial.

The difficulties associated with an effort to confirm, or confirm the unlikelihood of, a connection between Kbor Klib and the Battle of Zama are not insurmountable. Work is currently ongoing at the monument, in an effort to protect the structure from further water damage, and to stabilize especially weakened areas (Spring 2005). The central section of the east side in particular is in danger of collapse where excavations were earlier carried out (presumably at the time of the Prenat/Déroche investigation), as is a section further to the south, along the same face (*Figs. 61 & 62*). These clearances are already revealing features of the original configuration of monument not previously evident (*Fig. 63*). It is possible that the clearances associated with the drainage measures, as well as any re-opening or extension of the old excavations in order to introduce stabilized backfill, will produce securely datable materials confirming the chronology of Kbor Klib.

One of the aspects of the chronology proposed by Ferchiou was the paucity of ceramic evidence contributing to the stylistic evidence on which she consequently had to principally rely. A campaign especially focused on gathering ceramic material, consisting of a series of sensitively placed and backfilled sondages reaching undisturbed strata, might produce a sufficient body of identifiable shards to confirm an earlier or later date for Kbor Klib.

The architectural fragments recovered from Kbor Klib are still in storage in the Bardo museum in Tunis (*Fig. 64*). While acknowledging the painstaking evaluation of these elements carried out by Ferchiou, it would certainly be possible to solicit other opinions from specialists in the study of these types of components. An exercise to identify, assemble, photograph, catalogue and disseminate these fragments, using the Internet as the vehicle of dissemination, might stimulate sufficient discussion and debate to lead to consensus regarding their chronology.

Aspects of the configuration of Kbor Klib are still very much in doubt. With the possible difference in height of the three sections composing the monument, it is not entirely clear how the structure would have originally appeared. It is suggested that the central section would have been considerably higher than the approximately 85cm reflected in the current condition of the monument (Rakob 2005). Whatever the height difference of the center section, the frieze of arms will have been unlikely to have run at the same elevation along the entire east and west face. This makes more likely Ferchiou's speculation that the frieze might have only decorated the center section. A structure of differing heights also complicates determining a location of the columns remnants associated with the structure. Perhaps a minute examination of the paving around the structure, once cleared, would reveal evidence to indicate where these columns were located. Scrutiny of the upper sections of the monument might reveal traces of the frieze, or its method of connection, unnoticed by earlier investigators.

Fig. 60. Example of Roman battle trophy, consisting of armor mounted on a pole. (image taken from : http://www.vroma.org/~bmcmanus/romanarmy_images.html)

Fig. 61. Collapsing center section of east face, at old sondage.

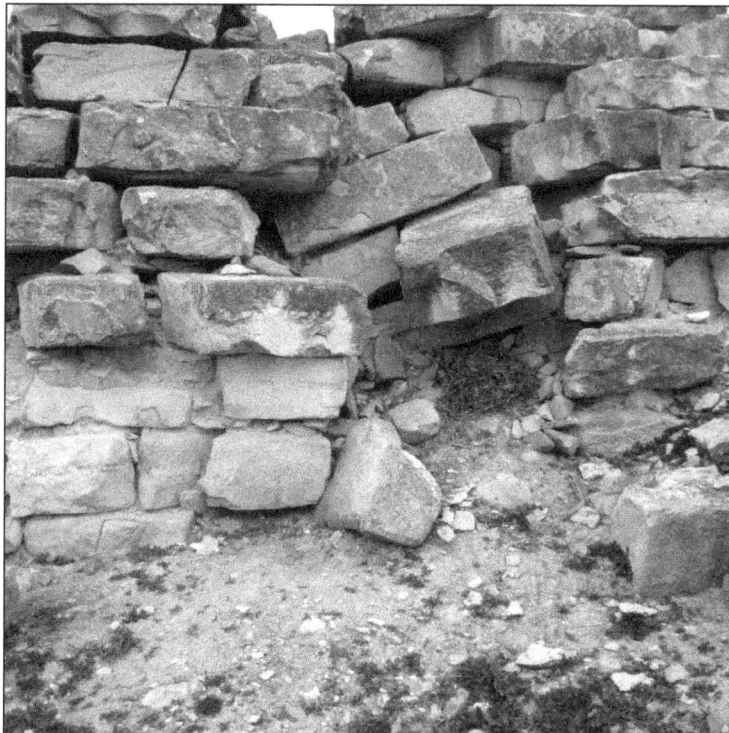

Fig. 62. Collapsing south portion of the east face, probably as the result of ancient stone robbing

Fig. 63. Ongoing clearances revealing extended paving around the north end of the monument.

For the battle, it is possible that traces remain. Aerial survey might, even at this late date, reveal signs of the Roman marching camp on the hill where it is proposed to have been located. Surface survey there and, if this produced results, excavation, might provide datable material. The fields where the battle is proposed to have been fought are agricultural, and have the appearance of having been so for some time. A campaign of field walking, perhaps combined with a metal detecting survey, might produce datable evidence. Interviews with the local inhabitants might produce reports of recovery of relics related to the battle, whether or not they would have been recognized as such. The modern researchers of the ancient accounts conclude that in excess of seventy thousand troops were probably involved in the battle, with over twenty thousand of those perishing in the conflict. It is certainly not outside the realm of possibility, particularly in this climate, on this terrain, that artifacts remain.

Ultimately no program of investigation might decide conclusively the function, chronology and reason for construction of Kbor Klib. It may be the case that for any study of this enigmatic monument, to quote Ferchiou, "l'état de dégradation du Kbor Klib ne permettra sans doute jamais de parvenir à des certitudes"

(1991: 75). Regardless of the potential for certainty, however, in respect of chronology, location, decoration, and the conditions pertaining in the Numidia of the period, any investigation must surely consider the possibility of a connection with the battle of Zama.

Fig. 64. Recent photograph of the Artemis bust, in storage in the Bardo museum.

Bibliography

Appian. *The Foreign Wars*, trans. H. White. Available online at:
http://www.perseus.tufts.edu/cgi-
bin/ptext?doc=Perseus%3Atext%3A1999.01.0230&layout=&loc=Trans.%20Pref.&query=toc.
(22 October 2003)

Ayachi, T. 2003. L'énigme Zama élucidée. *La Gazelle; le magazine de Tunis Air* 20: 36-37.

Belmont, J., Esteban, C. and Gonzalez, J. 1998. Mediterranean archaeoastronomy and archaeotopography:
Pre-Roman tombs of Africa Proconsularis. *Archaeoastronomy* 23: S7 – S24.

Bisi, A.M. 1971. Un naiskos tardo-Fenicio del museo di Beyrut e il problema dell'origine dei cippi
Egittizzanti nel mondo Punico. *Antiquités Africaines* 5: 15-38

Bouchenaki, M. 1979. Contribution à la connaissance de la Numidie avant la conquête romaine. In H. Horn
and C. Ruger (eds), *Die Numider: Reiter und Könige nördlich der Sahara.*
Koln: Rheinland-Verlag GmbH.

Brett, M. and Fentress, E. 1996. *The Berbers.* Oxford and Cambridge, Mass.: Blackwell.

Brunon, Le General. 1887. *Recherches sur le Champ de Bataille de Zama.* Montpellier: Charles Boehm.

Cagnat, R. and Saladin, H. 1887. Voyage en Tunisie. In Charton, E. (ed.) *Le Tour du Monde.*
Paris: Hachette.

Cagnat, R. and Merlin, A. 1920. *Atlas archeologique de la Tunisie*, Deuxieme Serie – 2e Livraison,
"Maktar". Paris: Editions Ernest Leroux.

Camp, J. et al. 1992. A Trophy from the Battle of Chaironeia of 86 B.C. *American Journal of Archaeology.*
Abstract available online at:
http://www.ajaonline.org/archive/96.3/camp_john_michael_ie.html. (21 December 2004)

Camps, G. 1960. Massinissa ou les debuts de l'histoire. *Libyca* 8, 1er Semestre.

Camps, G. 1961. *Aux origines de la Berbérie: monuments et rites funéraires protohistoriques.*
Paris: Arts et Métiers Graphiques.

Camps, G. 1979. Les Numides et la Civilisation Punique. *Antiquités Africaines* 14: 43-53

Cassius Dio. *Roman History.* Loeb Classical Library. Available online at:
http://www.ukans.edu/history/index/europe/ancient_rome/E/Roman/Texts/Cassius_Dio/home.html.
(19 November 2003)

Coarelli, F. and Thébert, Y. 1988. Architecture funéraire et pouvoir: reflexions sur l'hellénisme Numide.
Mélanges d'archéologie et d'histoire de l'école Française de Rome, antiquité 100-2: 761-818.

Cottrell, L. 1960. *Enemy of Rome.* London: Evans Brothers Limited.

Déroche, L. 1948. Les fouilles de Ksar Toual Zammel et la question de Zama.
Mélanges d'archéologie et d'histoire de l'école Française de Rome LX: 55-104.

Déroche, L. 1949. Comptes rendus des séances de l'année 1949. *Comptes rendus des séances de
l'académie des inscriptions & belles-lettres* Janvier-Mars: 231-232.

Encyclopædia Britannica, The New, 15th Edition, Volume 12, Micropædia, 2002. Zama, Battle of.

Ennabli, A. Zama ("Aelia Hadriana Augusta") Tunisia. *The Princeton Encyclopedia of Classical Sites*
(eds Richard Stillwell, William L. MacDonald, Marian Holland McAllister). Available online at:
http://www.perseus.tufts.edu/cgi-
bin/ptext?doc=Perseus%3Atext%3A1999.04.0006%3Aid%3Dzama.
(04 February 2004)

EurNews, 14 Marzo 2002, "La scoperta", Online article describing Zama Regia incription discovery at:
http://www.02-1.eurnews.it/marzo/restodelcarlino15.htm. (07 October 2003)

Fentress, E.W.B. 1979. *Numidia and the Roman Army.* Oxford: B.A.R.

Ferchiou, N. 1991. Le Kbor Klib. *Quaderni di Archeologia della Libia* 14: 45-97.

Ferjaoui, A. 2001. Recherches archéologiques et toponymiques sur le site de Jama et dans ses alentours.
Comptes rendus des séances de l'académie des inscriptions & belles-lettres Avr-Oct: 837-864.

Ferjaoui, A. 2002. Localisation de Zama Regia a Jama. *Comptes rendus des séances de l'académie des
inscriptions & belles-lettres* Juillet-Octobre: 1004-1017.

Frank, T. 1926. The Inscriptions of the Imperial Domains of Africa. *The American Journal of Philology*
47-1: 55-73

Garcia-Bellido, M. P. 1998. Sobre la Identificacion de Dea Caelestis en Monumentos del Museo del

Bardo (Tunez). In *Actas del Congreso "El Mediterraneo en la Antiguedad: Oriente y Occidente"*, *Sapanu*.
Publicaciones en Internet II. Available online at:
http://www.labherm.filol.csic.es/Sapanu1998/Es/Actas/GarcBell/MpazGB.htm.
(25 September 2003)

Gatopoulos, D. 2004. Greek farmer finds 2,000-year-old monument. *Associated Press*.
Available online at:
http://seattlepi.nwsource.com/national/apeurope_story.asp?category=1103&slug=Greece%20Ancient%20Monument (21 December 2004)

Ghaki, M. 2004. Personal Correspondence. December 2004.

Goldsworthy, A. 2000. *The Punic Wars*. London: Cassell & Co.

Jacobs, D. & Morris, P. 2001. *The Rough Guide to Tunisia*. London: Rough Guides Ltd

Knight, K. 2003. *Catholic Encyclopedia, The*. Volume XV. Zama. Available online at:
http://www.newadvent.org/cathen/15746b.htm. (21 March 2004)

Kromayer, J. and Veith, G. 1912. *Antike Schlachtfelder*, 2, in Italien und Afrika. Berlin: Weidmannsche Buchhandlung.

Kromayer, J. and Veith, G. 1922. *Schlachten-Atlas zur Antiken Kriegsgeschichte*, Römische Abteilung, 2, von Cannae bis Numantia. Leipzig: H. Wagner & E. Debes.

Lancel, S. 1995. *Hannibal*. Translated by Antonia Nevill. 1998. Oxford: Blackwell Publishers Ltd.

Lazenby, J.F. 1998. *Hannibal's war: a military history of the Second Punic War*. Norman: University of Oklahoma Press.

Lézine, A. 1956. La Maison des chapiteaux histories a Utique.
Karthago: revue trimestrielle d'archéologie africaine. VII: 1-33.

Lézine, A. 1962. *Architecture Punique*. Publications de l'Université de Tunis.

Lézine, A. 1968. Note sur le Kbour Klib. *Carthage . Utique: etudes d'achitecture et d'urbanisme*. Paris: Editions du Centre National de la Recherche Scientifique

Livy. *History of Rome: Book 30*, trans. Rev. C. Roberts, Everyman's Library, The History of Rome, Vol. 4. London: J. M. Dent & Sons. Available online at:
http://mcadams.posc.mu.edu/txt/ah/Livy/Livy30.html. (10 October 2003)

M'charek, A. 1991. Inscriptions découvertes entre *Zama Regia* (Henchir Jâma) et *[Ma]rag(ui) Sara* (Henchir Chaâr). *L'Africa romana* 9-1: 252-264.

Merlin, A. 1944. *Inscriptions latines de la Tunisie*. Paris: Presses Universitaires de France.

Mommsen, T. 1856. *History of Rome, Volume III*. Translated by William Purdie Dickson. 1894.
Available online at: http://www.gutenberg.net/1/0/7/0/10703/10703.txt. (14 May 2004)
(note: online version does not contain page numbers)

Moscati, S. (ed.) 1997. *The Phoenicians*. London: I.B.Tauris & Co Ltd

Moscati, S. 1986. Le Stele di Sulci: Caratterie & Confronti. *Collezione di Studi Fenici* 23. Roma: Consiglio Nazionale delle Ricerche

Nepos, Cornelius. *Lives of Eminent Commanders: Hannibal*, ed. Roger Pearse. Available online at:
http://www.ccel.org/p/pearse/morefathers/nepos_eintro.htm. (18 October 2003)

Pareti, L. Zama. *Atti della Royale Accademia delle Scienze di Torino*, 46. 1910-1911 : 302-327.

Picard, G. Ch. 1947. Séance de la commission de l'Afrique du nord. *Bulletin archéologique du comité des travaux historiques et scientifiques* Annees 1946-1947-1948-1949.
10 Fevrier 1947: 229, & 8 Décembre 1947: 375-376.

Picard, G. Ch. 1948. Les Monuments triomphaux Romains en Afrique. *Comptes rendus des séances de l'académie des inscriptions & belles-lettres* Janvier-Avril: 421-427.

Picard, G. Ch. 1951. Archaeological News. *American Journal of Archaeology* 55: 192-193.

Picard, G. Ch. 1957. *Les trophees romains: contribution a l'histoire de la religion et de l'art triomphal de Rome*.
Paris: E. De Boccard.

Picard, G. Ch. 1959. Les Fouilles de la Via del Mare et les débuts de l'art triomphal Romain. *Mélanges d'archéologie et d'histoire de l'école Française de Rome* LXXI: 263-288.

Picard, G. Ch. 1963. Pagus Thuscae et Gunzuzi. *Comptes rendus des séances de l'académie des inscriptions & belles-lettres* Janvier-Mars: 124-130.

Picard, G. Ch. 1967. *Hannibal*. Paris: Hachette.

Picard, C. & Picard, G. Ch. 1980. Recherches sur l'architecture Numide. *Karthago: revue d'archéologie africaine*. XIX: 16-31.

Picard, Gilbert-Charles, Obituary of. 1999. *Antiquités Africaines* 35: 5-19.

Pietilä-Castrén, L. 1987. Magnificentia publica: The Victory Monuments of the Roman Generals in the Era of the Punic Wars. *Commentationes Humanarum Litterarum* 84: 154-158.

Pliny the Elder. *The Natural History*. eds Bostock, J. and Riley, H.T. 1855. London: Taylor and Francis. Available online at:

http://www.perseus.tufts.edu/cgi-bin/ptext?doc=Perseus%3Atext%3A1999.02.0137

Polito, E. 1999. Emblèmes Macédoniens. Une hypothèse sur une série de boucliers de Macédoine en Numidie. *Antiquités Africaines* 35: 39-70.

Polybius. *The Histories*, Loeb Classical Library. Available online at: http://www.ku.edu/history/index/europe/ancient_rome/E/Roman/Texts/Polybius/15*.html. (05 October 2003)

Quinn, J.C. 2003. *Roman Africa?* Digressus Supplement 1. Available online at: http://www.digressus.org. (27 September 2003)

Rakob, F. 1979a. Numidische Königsarchitektur in Nordafrika. In H. Horn and C. Ruger (eds), *Die Numider: Reiter und Könige nördlich der Sahara*. Koln: Rheinland-Verlag GmbH.

Rakob, F. 1979b. Modell des numidischen Höhenheiligtums von Chemtou/Tunesien. In H. Horn and C. Ruger (eds), *Die Numider: Reiter und Könige nördlich der Sahara*. Koln: Rheinland-Verlag GmbH.

Rakob, F. 1994. *Simitthus, 2: Der Tempelberg und das Römische Lager*. Mainz: Philipp Von Zabern.

Rakob, F. 2005. Personal Conversation. 06 February 2005. DKV Residenz am Tibusplatz, Münster, Germany

Raven, S. 1984. *Rome in Africa*. London and New York: Longman.

Ribichini, S. 1997. Beliefs and Religious Life. In Moscati, S. (ed.) *The Phoenicians*. London: I.B.Tauris & Co Ltd.

Russell, F. 1970. The Battlefield of Zama. *Archaeology* 23-2: 120-129.

Sallust. *The Jugurthine War*, ed. Rev. John Selby Watson. 1899. London: Harper & Brothers. Available online at: http://www.perseus.tufts.edu/cgi-bin/ptext?doc=Perseus%3Atext%3A1999.02.0126. (12 November 2003)

Saumagne, C. 1941. Zama Regia. *Revue Tunisienne*. 235-269.

Scullard, H.H. 1970. *Scipio Africanus: Soldier and Politician*. London: Thames & Hudson.

Seibert, J. 2004. Hannibal als Feldherr. In Badisches Landesmuseum Karlsruhe, *Hannibal ad portas: Macht und Reichtum Karthagos*. Stuttgart: Konrad Theiss Verlag GmbH

Siebold, J. 1998. Tabula Peutingeriana, Slide #120, Monograph. *Cartographic Images*. Available online at: http://www.henry-davis.com/MAPS/Ancient%20Web%20Pages/120mono.html. (01 February 2004)

Smith, W. (ed). 1854. *Dictionary of Greek and Roman Geography*. Available online at: http://www.perseus.tufts.edu/cgi-bin/ptext?doc=Perseus%3Atext%3A1999.04.0064%3Aid%3Dzama.

Strabo, *Geography*. Loeb Classical Library. Available online at: http://www.ukans.edu/history/index/europe/ancient_rome/E/Roman/Texts/Strabo/17C*.html (28 March 2004)

Talbert, R. (ed.). 2000. *Barrington Atlas of the Greek and Roman World*. Woodstock: Princeton University Press.

Vitruvius Pollio. *The Ten Books on Architecture*. Edited by Morris Hicky Morgan. Available online at: http://www.perseus.tufts.edu/cgi-bin/ptext?doc=Perseus%3Atext%3A1999.02.0073&query=doctitle%3D%231.

(14 December 2004)

Walbank, F.W. 1967. *A Historical Commentary on Polybius*, Vol II. Oxford: The Clarendon Press.

Walsh, P.G. 1965. Massinissa. *The Journal of Roman Studies* 55: 149-160.

Warmington, B.H. 1969. *Carthage*. London: Hale.

Warry, J. 1980. *Warfare in the Classical World*. London: Salamander Books.

Yates, J.A. Masinissa – Rome's Most Faithful Client King. Available online at:
http://www.barca.fsnet.co.uk/masinissa-client-king.htm. (22 February 2004)

WEBSITE IMAGES PROVENANCE

Fig. 28, Map of pre-Numidian North Africa, taken from:
http://www.barca.fsnet.co.uk/Graphics/map-north-africa.gif
(05 February 2004)

Fig.31, Portrait of Massinissa, taken from: http://www.barca.fsnet.co.uk/masinissa.htm
(20 February 2005)

Fig. 32. The Medracen, Massinissa's putative tomb, Algeria, taken from: http://www.visit-algeria.com
(10 June 2005) (©Mostefa BRAHIM/Agence Orianis)

Fig. 43a, Artemis head coin, taken from: http://www.athina.ch/GR/GR07/big88.htm
Macedon Under Roman Domination, 158 - 150 BC AR Tetradrachm. 16.77 g.,
Diademed head of Artemis right with quiver and bow, in center of Macedonian shield
decorated with stars. (05 February 2004)

Fig. 45, Peutinger Table section showing Zama Regia, taken from:
http://www.fh-augsburg.de/%7Eharsch/Chronologia/Lspost03/Tabula/tab_pe06.html
(20 February 2005)

Fig. 46, 50, 54, 56, and *57*, Maps, taken from: http://www.mapmart.com/Common/confirm.asp
(18 February 2005)

Fig. 51, Map of Battle of Zama, taken from: http://www.barca.fsnet.co.uk/zama.htm
(05 February 2004)

Fig. 60, Roman Battle Trophy, taken from: http://www.vroma.org/~bmcmanus/romanarmy_images.html
(18 February 2005)

www.ingramcontent.com/pod-product-compliance
Lightning Source LLC
Chambersburg PA
CBHW061303270326
41932CB00029B/3450